1998

University of St. Francis Library

W9-ADI-773

The Good News About Juvenile Justice

THE COMMONWEAL JUVENILE JUSTICE MONOGRAPH SERIES

This is the fourth in the Commonweal Research Institute's series of monographs on juvenile justice. The three previous reports include the following:

The CYA Report: Conditions of Life at the California Youth Authority.
Bodily Harm: The Pattern of Fear and Violence at the California Youth Authority.
Reforming the CYA: How to End Crowding, Diversify Treatment and Protect the Public without Spending More Money.

All four reports are available and may be ordered from Commonweal, P.O. Box 316, Bolinas, CA 94924.

THE GOOD NEWS ABOUT JUVENILE JUSTICE

*The Movement Away From
Large Institutions and Toward
Community-Based Services*

by Steve Lerner
with an Introduction by Allen Breed

COMMON KNOWLEDGE PRESS
Bolinas, California

Copyright © 1990 by Commonweal.
All rights reserved.

Commonweal Research Institute and Common Knowledge Press are components of
Commonweal, a center for service and
research in health and human ecology. Its
three major interests are: (1) at-risk children
and families; (2) patient-centered medicine
and health care; and (3) environmental security for a sustainable future. Commonweal,
founded in 1976, is a California nonprofit
corporation that has worked in health promotion for at-risk children and adults since its
inception. Its work has been supported by
grants and gifts from foundations and individ-
uals across the United States.

ACKNOWLEDGMENTS

This monograph was written for the
Commonweal Research Institute of Bolinas,
California. It was edited by Ellen Hoffman
of Washington, D.C., and by David Parker of
the Commonweal staff.
    The book was made possible by a grant
to Commonweal from the Ittleson Foundation of New York. The Commonweal CYA
Project has also received recent support from
the Edna McConnell Clark Foundation, the
Wallace A. Gerbode Foundation, the Luke B.
Hancock Foundation, the Public Welfare
Foundation, the Haigh-Scatena Foundation,
and the Heller Charitable and Educational
Fund. We hereby express our deep gratitude
to all those who have made our work on
behalf of CYA reform possible.

This report is available from Commonweal,
P.O. Box 316, Bolinas, CA 94924, and the
National Council on Crime and Delinquency,
685 Market Street, San Francisco, CA 94105,
for $5.95 plus $1.25 postage, prepaid. California residents add 37¢ sales tax.

Book design & production by Triad, San
Rafael, and typeset by TBD Typography.

ISBN 0-943004-05-5

First printing

Printed in the USA

364.6
L 615

Contents

Foreword

Opposing principles guide the development of juvenile justice policy in the United States. On the one hand, Americans believe that stern measures are needed to control youth crime. On the other hand, Americans believe that children should be treated differently from adults, and that some investment should be made in the rehabilitation of young people who break the law.

These conflicting attitudes have done war with each other since the turn of the century, when the juvenile justice system was created. In the decade just ended, the tough side of this divided mentality has dominated the public policy agenda. This toughness has produced a new body of laws and practices diminishing the traditional protections available to delinquent youth and emphasizing adult-like punishments. A prime example of the drift toward a less forgiving policy is the recent United States Supreme Court decision affirming the states' right to impose the death penalty on juveniles over the age of 16. In less dramatic terms, but affecting a far greater number of youths, new laws in some states have increased the flow of juveniles into state prisons, have expanded youth training school populations, and have lengthened sentences for youthful offenders.

The emergence of an "accountability" model of juvenile justice has been a disturbing development for many dedicated advocates and professionals who believe that a well-run and separate system of justice for youth can meet the goals established by the system's founders so many years ago. One of the dangers of our growing acceptance of the accountability model is that we may lose sight of the original and worthwhile goals of the juvenile justice system. Indeed, some critics of the system have already thrown in the towel and have called for its abandonment.

This treatise by Steve Lerner on model juvenile justice reform approaches comes at a critical time in the evolution of our separate system of justice for youth. What it contributes is a long-absent sense of optimism about what the system can do if it is cultivated and allowed to operate as intended.

Lerner provides us with a detailed analysis of how, in a few select states, policymakers have reiterated their support for the treatment-based goals of the juvenile justice system by investing in new programs and approaches that are proving to be effective in the control of future misconduct by young offenders. He describes the transformation of juvenile justice policy in Massachusetts, Pennsylvania, Utah, and Maryland. To varying degrees, each of these states closed large, prison-like institutions and developed, in the wake of the closures, community-based care systems for these youth. Lerner also gives us an account of developments in Florida, where some innovative new programs for serious youthful offenders have been established.

For those who have not had the opportunity to appreciate developments in the juvenile justice reform states, this book will provide an instructive overview of the deinstitutionalization experience. But the work is not limited to a survey course. It provides detailed information on youth programs that now serve as alternatives to institutions in the reform states. It also helps us to understand the political forces and decisions behind the transformation of juvenile justice systems in these bellwether states.

One valuable lesson emerging from this work is that the transformation of these juvenile justice systems did not occur quickly, or without pain. In each of the states studied, we learn that the process of replacing institutions with community-care networks has been controversial, slow, or plagued by mistakes along the way. In Massachusetts, for example, a 1976 legislative revolt against the training school closure threatened to end the experiment with deinstitutionalization. In Pennsylvania, union opposition to the transfer of services to private operators almost scuttled reform plans. In Utah, the community-contracting scheme went back to the drawing board when the cost of subsidizing empty beds became too high. And in Maryland today, plans to fund new community-based programs have been forced into competition with demands to add new institutional beds for youthful offenders.

Despite these setbacks, Lerner cites a record of significant achievement in each of the states reviewed. He also sees the accomplishments in the bellwether states as the harbinger of a wider reform movement. Lerner suggests that "we can begin to hear the sound of the ice breaking up as old ways of confining large numbers of delinquents in oversized, frequently brutal training schools are being challenged by new, more successful, and more humane approaches."

Hopefully Lerner is right in his estimate that the sense of innovation and enthusiasm coming out of the reform states will be catching. Certainly there is a need to focus the wealth of knowledge emerging from these states on other states that are suffering the effects of over-reliance on large, prison-like institutions for delinquent youth. California, with its huge, costly, and overcrowded training school system, comes to mind as the state that may have the most to learn from the examples described in the text.

This volume is the fourth in a series of juvenile justice treatises produced by Steve Lerner and his co-authors. Previous volumes have dealt with the California Youth Authority — beginning in 1982 with *The CYA Report* and leading to the 1988 publication of a volume entitled *Reforming the CYA*. In all, Lerner has created a body of work that represents a significant contribution to the literature of juvenile justice in America today. No less than the previous reports, this one invites us to question commonplace notions about what works to control misconduct by youth. Moreover, it offers constructive alternatives to the juvenile justice administrators and policymakers in troubled states — alternatives that deserve their most thoughtful consideration.

ALLEN BREED, Chairman of the Board of the National Council on Crime & Delinquency.
(From 1978 to 1983, Mr. Breed served as the Director of the National Institute of Corrections in Washington, D.C. From 1967 to 1976, Breed was Director of the California Youth Authority and Chairman of the Youth Authority Board.)

Introduction

When I tell friends I have been visiting programs for juvenile offenders in various states, many of them groan. More than once I have been asked: "Isn't that awfully depressing?" Surprisingly, the answer is "no."

Far from being depressing, the field of juvenile justice is full of hope. One can hear the sounds of the ice breaking up as old ways of confining large numbers of delinquents in oversized, often brutal training schools are challenged by new, more successful and more humane approaches. In state after state, antiquated training schools are being closed and replaced with a spectrum of small, community-based programs.

Ira M. Schwartz, former administrator of the federal Office of Juvenile Justice and Delinquency Prevention, has tracked this change in juvenile crime control strategies in a number of states. In his recently published book, *(In)justice for Juveniles: Rethinking the Best Interest of the Child,* Schwartz calculates that one or more training schools have been closed in at least eight states: Massachusetts, Maryland, Pennsylvania, Utah, Florida, Missouri, Oklahoma, and Kentucky.

Furthermore, according to Schwartz, since 1979, training school populations have been cut in half in Arkansas and Idaho. Other states where correctional officials are reducing their training school populations include Colorado, Delaware, Louisiana, and Oregon. Policymakers in Georgia and Virginia are seeking ways to expand their community-based programs in order to reduce the number of youth in training schools. Juvenile justice officials are also reexamining their approach to juvenile crime control in Hawaii, Ohio, Maine, Mississippi, Nevada, South Carolina, Tennessee, Rhode Island, Wisconsin, and Wyoming.[1]

Key States

This monograph focuses on the transformation of the juvenile justice system in four key states that have led the way in closing their training schools: Massachusetts, Utah, Pennsylvania, and Maryland. It also describes some developments in Florida where, despite an uneven record in juvenile justice reform, state officials have significantly reduced the training school population and encouraged the development of some innovative community-based programs.

The report takes a slightly different approach in looking at each state:

Massachusetts, the first state to shut down all of its training schools, has served as a national model. This chapter describes the conditions and events that led to closing of the schools, the resistance to reform, and the alternative programs that have emerged from 20 years of hard-fought reform.

Pennsylvania also closed its training school, but it retains a mix of state- and privately-run programs. Three alternatives to training schools established within the state are described: a nonprofit agency that operates a spectrum of small programs for delinquents; a 26-bed "last chance" facility operated by a for-profit company; and a large, unlocked, rural campus that has reduced intramural violence through the use of "positive peer pressure."

Utah has followed the Massachusetts example, and has enjoyed considerable success as a result. A vendor system under which the state purchases services from a network of private providers has prompted the development of a wide range of programs for delinquent youth. Recidivism studies suggest that the frequency and severity of delinquent behavior is reduced in graduates of Utah's community-based programs.

Maryland is still in the midst of reform. Officials have closed one training school and reduced the population at the last remaining large institution. While the political battle to reduce the training school population has been intense, correctional officials have managed to selectively transfer large numbers of juveniles out of training schools into community-based programs without jeopardizing public safety.

Florida has been forced to reduce its training school population under a consent decree stemming from a lawsuit. Political obstacles, however, have prevented continued investment in community-based alternatives. Furthermore, large numbers of juveniles continue to be sent to adult prisons. Nevertheless, some sophisticated, promising programs for delinquents have evolved and continue to flourish in the state.

Common Principles of Reform

Most of the states described in this report share some common assumptions and have instituted policies aimed at similar goals. Among these are the following:

• Committed youth should be held in the least restrictive environment possible.

• Rural training schools that confine large numbers of serious and lightweight offenders should be closed. Their large scale makes them difficult to manage; violence is endemic in most of them. Recidivism rates in training schools are also unacceptably high.

• Only about ten percent of the committed population requires secure confinement. Small, intensively-staffed, high-security facilities should be built for this population. The other 90 percent can be handled in community-based residential and non-residential programs.

• Small programs are preferable to large institutions, because staff workers have better control and can set and enforce standards for resident behavior. As a result, there is less violence in small programs that permit residents to shed their defensive posturing and concentrate on counseling and training.

• Wherever possible, these small programs should be located in residential areas. It is easier to effect the gradual release of a client back to his home from a community-based program than it is from an isolated rural institution.

• Other than a few high-security facilities reserved for serious offenders, community-based programs should be unlocked. Rather than depending on the hardware of incarceration, these programs should be made "staff-secure" through the use of non-incarcerative techniques for controlling client behavior.

• Programs for delinquents should do more than simply provide shelter and control their behavior. In addition to requiring that staff confront anti-social patterns of behavior, these programs should seek to encourage positive interactions between caring staff and delinquent youth.

• Private, nonprofit groups are capable of running successful community programs for juvenile offenders. Using a vendor system, states should contract with a wide variety of community groups that demonstrate talent for working with adjudicated young people. The state should monitor these programs closely, rewarding those that do well and closing those that do poorly.

• States should place a high priority on funding programs that help delinquents make the transition back to their community. In addition to the policing role of tracking young people once they return home, counselors should also be required to work as youth advocates, helping to create conditions that will allow their charges to succeed outside of an institutional framework.

Approaches that Work

In the states visited for this report, the once-fashionable, defeatist attitude that rehabilitating delinquents is impossible has been abandoned. In its place a new optimism is emerging. Staff workers at small programs targeted at delinquent populations with specific problems are finding that, while they are unable to heal the wounds of all the young people with whom they work, enough respond positively to counseling to make the effort worthwhile.

Common program components in good community-based programs include an academic regimen designed to upgrade the youth's educational status; drug and alcohol counseling; sex education; and instruction in how to locate, apply for, and keep a job.

In the most effective programs, delinquents are counseled in groups small enough to allow staff workers to set the tone and prevent residents from threatening or hurting each other. Once an atmosphere of safety has been established, youth and staff can focus their energy on improving a resident's academic skills and providing relevant vocational training that can lead to a real job for a youth who might otherwise never secure legal employment. When they graduate from the community-based, residential programs and return home, residents are gradually released into highly supervised probation programs to improve their chances of remaining crime-free.

Techniques for Working with Delinquents

Rehabilitating adolescents who have a lengthy criminal history and confirmed anti-social patterns of behavior is hard work that requires patience and perseverance. Good community-based programs evolve their own set of techniques for working with difficult adolescents. However, some common techniques turned up in the programs visited in the course of preparing this report.

To begin with, when a delinquent first comes to a program he is taught a few simple rules of behavior such as no fighting, no drugs or alcohol, no running away, no treating other residents or members of the staff with disrespect. A newcomer is assigned both a staff advisor and a resident role model to help him adjust to the program.

Subsequently, a new resident meets with members of the staff to set short- and long-term goals, so that it is apparent whether the delinquent is making progress or just killing time.

The real work begins the first time a resident tries to get his way through intimidation or manipulation. To the resident's surprise, his disruptive behavior is confronted not only by members of the staff, but also by other residents. From that point on, "positive peer pressure" is brought to bear on him.

If a resident refuses to go along with the program, he is taken aside by a counselor and "shadowed" until he is willing to behave. Short-term sanctions — such as assignment to work duty during leisure time — are also imposed to control impulsive behavior.

But all is not rules and punishments. The resident also receives tangible rewards — e.g., dinner in a restaurant or the opportunity to buy a T-shirt — which he can earn with "points" or "tokens" for good behavior.

The high staff-to-resident ratio also allows for intensive, one-on-one counseling in how to express personal feelings appropriately, without acting out. With his counselor, a resident can explore the causes of past anti-social behavior and develop a more positive self-image.

As a resident prepares to graduate, a number of home visits are arranged. An effort is made either to find him a job or to enroll him in school. In addition, there are counseling sessions with his family, during which sources of domestic tension are explored and rules for living at home are established. Finally, when the youth returns home, he is transferred to a highly supervised, non-residential program.

Some of these techniques have been tried with little success in large-scale training schools, where negative peer pressure generated by youth gangs has proven more potent than any counseling that the staff can provide. But when these counseling methods are consistently applied in small, community-based programs, they appear to be much more effective.

To tout this approach as a panacea for youth crime would be naive. No one claims that delinquency can be "cured," nor that all young people who attend or even complete the new rehabilitation programs will never commit another crime. The mere fact that a program is community-based does not ensure it will be either high quality or successful. Community-based programs can be only as effective as the people who design and run them.

However, despite these caveats and despite the limitations of available statistics, there is evidence that these programs offer hope. In some states where the delinquents are held in small, well-run, adequately funded, community-based programs there are signs that recidivism rates are declining. Even when young people are rearrested following their release from these community-based programs, generally they have committed less serious offenses than those for which they were previously found guilty. This promising recidivism data, and the so-called crime "suppression effect" attributed to community-based programs, are still preliminary and will no doubt continue to be hotly debated for years to come.

Even so, in the field of juvenile justice there is a growing consensus that recidivism rates in community-based systems are, at a very minimum, no worse than those generated by the training school systems; and that small, privately-run, residential programs are considerably more humane and less violent than large, difficult-to-control training schools.

What Causes Reform to Occur

The shift away from the training school model toward community-based programs appears to be percolating up from the bottom in states that have long been grappling with the dangers inherent in consigning large numbers of delinquents to training schools.

The shift seems to be occurring despite the lack of any concerted federal leadership, initiative, or funding.

As emerges from the experience of states profiled in this monograph, lawsuits, media exposés and financial pressures on state budgets appear repeatedly as factors that have propelled the closing of training schools and the development of alternatives across the country.

Sadly, tragedies such as the rape or suicide of an institutionalized youth have also instigated investigations that have led to the closing of training schools. In a number of instances these suicides are hauntingly similar.

A boy of 14 or 15 who has been confined in a training school for a property offense may come under intense pressure from older, more disturbed residents. Unable to stand up to his tormentors, the boy kills himself. Subsequently, the suicide is widely reported and advocacy groups swing into action calling for an investigation and reform of the system. In some cases lawsuits are brought.

Under pressure, state correctional officials and state legislators step back and look at the big picture. Task forces are formed and teams of inspectors are dispatched to the training school. Note is taken of the institution's long history of inmate-against-inmate violence. Task force members realize that, far from becoming rehabilitated, many of those who are committed to these institutions are surrounded by negative peer pressure to remain delinquent. The recidivism rates, sometimes as high as 70 or 80 percent, demonstrate the inefficacy of the training school as a long-term crime control mechanism.

Even in states where the political climate opposes the closing of training schools and placement of juveniles in community settings, financial pressures may speed the process. Faced with overcrowded facilities and judges who are handing down long sentences, many states must choose between building more training schools and adopting a new strategy. Constructing and operating high-security training schools for large numbers of delinquents, many of them property offenders not deemed to be dangerous or violent, is an expensive proposition.

In this context, alternative crime control strategies become more attractive. Policymakers discover the advantages of a reformed system that is more discriminating and places only a small number of chronic and violent offenders in high-security facilities. They realize that the remaining youths can be handled at least as effectively in small, staff-secure, community-based programs or intensive probation — either of which is less expensive than the bricks-and-mortar and operational costs of building and maintaining large institutions.

State officials also enjoy more flexibility and more control when they fund a network of private, nonprofit (or even profit-making) programs. If a program is deemed to be inhumane, inefficient, or unnecessary, the state administrator can simply discontinue its funding.

Opposition to Reform

While the logic sketched above seems compelling, and would lead many to conclude that large training schools should be closed, there remain concerns that public safety may be compromised in a community-based correctional system.

The strongest argument of supporters of training schools is that while these institutions may not be humane, they are nevertheless necessary to incapacitate young people who have committed serious crimes and who represent a danger to the public. Community-based systems, they contend, are nothing more than a "revolving door" that allows dangerous delinquents back onto the streets too rapidly without imposing on them adequate sanctions.

Correctional officials in states that have closed their training schools and opened community-based programs dispute this charge, arguing that there is no evidence that the public is in any greater danger from youths participating in the innovative programs. In fact, they assert, the public is safer under a community-based system than it is from a training school system that warehouses young people in a violent atmosphere for years and then releases them into society with few supports.

At the core of the debate is the difficult question of whether correctional officials can successfully differentiate between delinquents who are so dangerous that they must be locked up, and those who can be safely confined and counseled in less secure, community-based programs.

On this issue the two sides have established positions. Proponents of training schools contend that most young people who commit crimes should do time in locked facilities. The other side wants a strict definition of who needs to be incarcerated so that the majority of delinquents can be treated in community programs conducive to rehabilitation.

In the 1980s the political climate has favored those who wanted to incarcerate a large portion of the adjudicated population in locked facilities. State legislators have competed to prove that they are "tough on crime," passing laws that send more delinquents to secure facilities for longer periods of time for lesser and lesser crimes. Judges have handed

down stiffer sentences. Parole agents have found reasons to keep delinquents confined for longer periods. And correctional officials have pushed
to build more training schools to accommodate the rising numbers of
confined juveniles. Their chief focus has been to control the large numbers of committed young people in their reformatories rather than
to seek innovative ways of diverting the less serious offenders to less
secure programs.

This approach has been exemplified by California, which continues
to invest in a system that depends heavily on large training schools. The
California Youth Authority reports that on June 30, 1989, it confined
8,939 youths in training schools. No other state came close to matching
this figure. The next highest use of training schools was in Ohio, where
1,783 young people were incarcerated in institutions. In contrast, on
that same date, Massachusetts, with a population about one-fourth of
California's, had only 171 youths confined in small, high-security units.[2]

Swimming Upstream

While progress has been made in closing training schools in some
parts of the country, in other areas they have proven remarkably durable
despite evidence of intramural violence and high recidivism rates. One
reason for this is that powerful employee unions sometimes block the
closing of a facility. Merchants in communities where training schools
are located, as well as suppliers, can also wield considerable political
clout in keeping institutions open.

In addition, politicians have found it easy to play on their con-
stituents' fears about juvenile crime in an effort to keep training schools
open. In the last decade, the debate over appropriate sanctions for
juvenile offenders has often taken place at a very crude level. When the
subject arises in a political context, alternatives to training schools are
often dismissed as unsafe or too lenient. Candidates for public office
find it expedient to call for stricter sanctions for juvenile offenders,
rather than to engage in a more sophisticated discussion about which
crime control strategies are most humane, efficient, and cost-effective.

A Growing Trend

Despite a political climate that has been largely hostile to alternatives to incarceration, a good number of states have revamped their
juvenile justice systems, scrapped the training schools, and created a
variety of programs that allow judges to match the needs of the juvenile
to a program designed to meet those needs.

These community-based programs will no doubt turn out to have
their own weaknesses. They are of varied quality and some of them are

18

badly run. A few delinquents will, no doubt, learn how to manipulate the community-based system and escape serious sanctions for their wrong-doing. But with all these potential deficits, the community-based system still shows greater promise than the training schools that have failed so miserably.

What is exciting about the community-based reform movement is that it strikes at the very root of many of our social problems.

Those who attempt to rehabilitate delinquents inevitably must confront a spectrum of social ills that contribute to delinquency, including poverty, the breakdown of the family, poor-quality schools, and the widespread use of drugs. While staff of community-based programs obviously cannot solve these problems, they can advocate for their clients and help them cope more effectively with adverse circumstances. Unlike most training schools, community-based programs have a re-entry component that allows correctional workers to grapple with and sometimes to resolve some of the causes of delinquency.

For example, if a youth is running with the wrong crowd or has inadequate supervision at home, a reentry worker at a community-based program can help his client bring structure to his life and teach him how to reject negative peer pressure. If a client attends an inferior school and is on the verge of dropping out, the staff can find a remedial class for him where he will get more individual attention. If a client is abused at home, a foster home can be found. If the problem is inadequate housing, medical care, or food, workers can help the family negotiate the welfare system. If a client is a chronic thief, they can help him land a job and learn legitimate ways of making money. And if a client is convicted of substance abuse, they can teach him ways to enjoy life without getting high.

None of this is easy, and practitioners need to hear about programs and techniques that work. Fortunately, as the new wave of reform in juvenile justice continues to gather momentum around the country, workers on the front lines of this movement are beginning to compare notes. Word gets around about where the good programs are located. Gradually, an informal network of practitioners of this new art is coming together.

This monograph focuses on what works in the field of juvenile justice. Rather than continue to document the scandalous conditions in some state training schools, it describes programs that, in one form or another, show promise. It seeks to give the reader a glimpse into the workings of some of these new community-based programs, as well as an idea of how they evolved.

It is the hope of the author that this pamphlet will be useful to people in those state systems still dominated by training schools who want to help bring into being a more humane and effective system of caring for troubled young people.

---

[1]Schwartz, Ira M., *(In)justice for Juveniles: Rethinking the Best Interests of the Child,* Lexington Books, Lexington, Massachusetts, 1989.

[2]American Correctional Association, *Vital Statistics in Corrections,* Laurel, Maryland, 1989, p. 48.

Massachusetts Closes its Training Schools and Leads the Nation in a Shift to Community-based Programs

The juvenile justice system in Massachusetts today is among the best in the country. Correctional officials from some 35 states have made the pilgrimage to Boston to see if there are lessons they can learn from the bold transformation carried out by the Massachusetts Department of Youth Services (DYS).

What attracts them is a growing recognition that Massachusetts has created a more humane system of juvenile justice without compromising public safety. Incarcerating no more than ten percent of its committed youth in secure facilities, DYS has closed its training schools and built a broad spectrum of community-based, residential and non-residential programs for the rest of the young men and women committed to its care.

The evolution of this system, however, has not been without trauma. An account of the 20-year history of Massachusetts' journey from a training school-based system to a community-based system is both an inspirational and a cautionary tale: there are accomplishments to be admired and pitfalls to be avoided.

This chapter recounts the launching and development of the reform movement, describes the components of the Massachusetts system today, and examines several issues on the state's unfinished agenda.

LAUNCHING A MOVEMENT

The movement toward reform of the juvenile justice system in this country took a giant step forward in Massachusetts in 1970.

In a sense this was only fitting. A century and a quarter earlier, Massachusetts pioneered reforms in juvenile justice as the first state in the nation to segregate juvenile offenders from adults by isolating them in rural reformatories.

21

Separating adjudicated delinquents from the rough-and-tumble of adult jails in 1847 was a compassionate reform. Since then, however, the new reformatories, now called "training schools," have developed deep flaws of their own. Rather than evolving into the envisioned sanctuaries for rehabilitation, these facilities became dangerous and oppressive places where young people were frequently brutalized.

Yitzhak Bakal, a former Assistant Commissioner of DYS, has little good to say about the training schools he once helped administer. "The treatment of youths inside the institutions was at best custodial and at worst punitive and repressive. Marching, shaved heads, and enforced periods of long silences were regular occurrences. Punitive staff used force and made recalcitrant children drink water from toilets, or scrub floors on their hands and knees for hours on end. Solitary confinement was also used extensively and rationalized as a mode of treatment for those who needed it," he writes.[1]

The training schools became "dumping grounds," or catch-all repositories for a wide variety of young people who had run afoul of the law. Judges used them almost indiscriminately because there were very few other options for placement. As a result, "lightweight" offenders were regularly committed to training schools along with the more serious, violent offenders. Not surprisingly, the former were frequently victimized by the latter. Too often, young people were beaten and sexually assaulted by older, tougher inmates.[2]

Frequently referred to as "human warehouses" or "academies of crime," Massachusetts training schools were also more custodial in nature than treatment-oriented. Staff composition reflected this bias for control over treatment: custodial staff outnumbered the clinical staff by 22 to 1, Bakal writes. The training school system had the effect of teaching young people institutionalized patterns of behavior by isolating them from their families and communities. Their treatment in these facilities confirmed for them their self-image as "delinquents."

Over the years, training schools proliferated across the country as the institutional answer to adolescent crime. In 1965 there were 220 training schools with a capacity of 42,423. A 70 percent increase was expected by 1975.[3] In Massachusetts there were five: The Lyman School for Boys, the Shirley Industrial School for Boys, the Oakdale Residential Treatment Unit, the Lancaster Industrial School for Girls, and a maximum security unit called the Bridgewater Guidance Center.

By the mid-1960s a near "pathological state" existed in Massachusetts training schools, Bakal writes. The pattern of abuses in these facilities became so blatant that pressure for reform mounted from the media, the legislature, and professional groups. A series of scathing reports about the weakness and abuses inherent in the system culminated in the resignation in 1969 of Dr. John Coughlin, director of the Division of Youth Services (DYS), then responsible for the administration of the youth corrections system.

Shortly thereafter, the state legislature passed a law giving the new director of DYS broad powers to "establish necessary facilities for detention, diagnosis, treatment, and training of its charges including post-release care." Known as the "Reorganization Act," the legislation redefined the mission of DYS in terms of "therapy, prevention, community services, purchase of services and research."[4]

The members of the Massachusetts legislature might have trod more carefully had they realized that calling for these seemingly sober and innocuous reforms would lead the state into the most radical experiment in the deinstitutionalization of juvenile offenders in the history of the nation. As it was, however, the stage was set for a new director to take up an unprecedented mandate to reform juvenile justice practices.

Pressure for reform may also have been exerted through informal political channels. A persistent rumor suggests that Governor Francis Sargent's wife played a key role in bringing about the transformation of the Massachusetts system of juvenile justice. It is said that on a tour of a training school, Mrs. Sargent witnessed a resident being beaten and subsequently asked her husband to do something about it.

Enter Jerome Miller, who was to become the nation's leading advocate and practitioner of closing large training schools and opening a spectrum of small, nonprofit, community-based halfway houses and non-residential programs. Appointed as the first Commissioner of the DYS by Governor Sargent in October, 1969, Miller had previously developed an innovative youth service agency for dependents of the U.S. Air Force and had served as an associate professor at Ohio State University School of Social Work.

The timing of Miller's appointment could not have been more propitious. The governor was in favor of reform. The Legislature had passed the Reorganization Act giving him broad powers to pursue reform. And there had been a spate of reports and media exposés that predisposed public opinion in favor of substantial reforms.

Yet despite these advantages, Miller faced a daunting task. Abuses at the training schools were widespread and the bureaucracy was resistant to change. As he soon learned, it was one thing to be the appointed commissioner of juvenile justice; it was quite another to ensure that his new policies were actually carried out.

"When I arrived there it was a political patronage system," Miller recalls. "Some 90 percent of the correctional employees were there through political patronage, not through the civil service. So by taking on the institutions I was taking on the politicians' power base."

Unfixable Facilities

Miller did not set out to close Massachusetts training schools. First he tried to fix them. Borrowing from the British, he brought in experts to establish a "therapeutic community" approach to rehabilitation within the training school environment. The idea was to do away with the heavy-handed guard/inmate relationship in which the guard gave the orders and the inmate was supposed to be submissive. Under the new regime, an effort was made to equalize the relationship so that "clients" could be resocialized by "counselors."

Not surprisingly, these initiatives provoked a staff revolt, reports Bakal, who was one of Miller's handpicked assistant commissioners. Many senior staff thought that Miller's ideas were undermining their authority, making it impossible to control the institutions. Staff sabotage of the new reforms caused mass escapes and other breakdowns of institutional order to occur. But rather than retreat from his position, Miller went on the offensive. He prohibited training school staff from hitting their charges and discouraged the excessive use of disciplinary lock-up. Furthermore, he went public with his problems, sometimes appearing before the press or on lecture tours with inmates who told about abuses in the training schools. Instead of hiding the problems he faced, Miller opened up the process and appealed for public support.

Aware that there was a limit to his ability to reform the large training schools, Miller closed the maximum security unit at Bridgewater in 1970 and began to phase out the training school at Shirley in 1971. It was not until January, 1972, that Miller gave up on the training school model altogether as inherently corrupting and dysfunctional. While the legislature was out of session, he closed the remaining facilities — including the infamous, 630-bed Lyman School for Boys, the oldest reformatory in the country, opened in 1846.

To say that Miller's decision to close the training schools came unexpectedly would be an understatement. While it was widely understood that training schools were not rehabilitating young people and that the schools were prone to abuse, even critics of the training school model pointed out that there were few alternatives available. To close all the training schools at the same time, without adequate alternatives in place, was considered ill-advised by many. Where would the young criminals go?[5] But Miller had reached a point where he felt the only way to create a network of alternative programs was to cause an immediate demand for them. Once he had closed the training schools, there was no more room for debate. New programs were needed immediately.

"After initial staff bewilderment and surprise, energies were released toward the creation of community-based alternatives," writes Bakal. With only a few alternative programs available, 100 youths stayed on the University of Massachusetts campus for a month while slots were created for them in community-based programs. Detention centers, forestry camps, and Outward Bound programs absorbed others. The most serious, hard-core delinquents were placed at Andros, a new, small, high-security, intensive-care unit established in Roslindale.

By the time the dust settled, programs had been found for the 1,200 youths committed each year to DYS in the early 1970s. Only five percent were confined in high-security facilities. Some 600 were sent home and received with outreach and tracking services that provided them with one person to counsel and advocate for them and another to closely monitor their behavior. Approximately 500 were dispersed among a growing network of group homes. The rest were placed in foster homes or specialized residential placements such as psychiatric hospitals or private schools.

A Period of Creative Chaos

From all accounts, considerable turmoil and chaos accompanied this swift program of deinstitutionalization. Looking back on this period, Miller's critics suggest that he should have done more planning and had more alternative programs available before closing the training schools. Others believe that Miller's preemptive strike made it impossible for opposition forces to coalesce and become organized. By closing the training schools, Miller presented his opponents with a fait accompli — easy to criticize, but hard to undo.

Miller was also criticized for not opening enough locked facilities for dangerous young people. In his own defense, Miller says he does not regret having argued for as few secure beds as possible. In fact, he characterizes the expansion of locked facilities that occurred after his tenure as ill-advised. "There is a ten-year evaluation by the Harvard Center for Criminal Justice that says we didn't go far enough, that even the most disturbed kids could have been handled in smaller homes in groups of two or three.[6] The report also says we relied too much on group homes instead of individual treatment," Miller says by way of answering his critics.

"There really are not as many violent kids as you would think. We would get four to eight murderers a year when I was commissioner. If you include those coming in for aggravated assault or rape, where someone is badly hurt, I don't think you would get more than 35 or 40."

While Miller takes a strong position on severely limiting the number of young people in high-security facilities, he concedes that some delinquents are too dangerous to handle in an unlocked environment. "Those few kids who are dangerous and hurt people should be in small facilities with a minimum of hardware that you try to make as humane and undebilitating as possible."

In arguing for as few of these locked facilities as possible, Miller saw himself as bargaining for the best deal he could get, given the political realities. "I realized that I would lose the debate for 35–40 secure beds and that we would end up with 70, but if I had started by arguing for 125, I'd have ended up with 300," he explains.

Miller argues against placing young people who are chronic property offenders in locked facilities. "If a kid is a career offender you want to shower him with services. Incapacitate him not by locking him up but by having someone out on the street with him monitoring his every move," he continues.

Responding to those who say that such an approach is mollycoddling criminals, Miller notes that, ironically, delinquents are much more aggravated by social workers and counselors constantly making demands on them and confronting them than they are by locked facilities. "If you want your pound of flesh from these kids, do it with a little love. These violent kids can do a stint in a locked institution standing on their ear. But they can't stand the caring, bleeding-heart programs."

The Movement Becomes a System

While Jerome Miller started a revolution or a movement in juvenile justice, it fell to those who followed him to consolidate the community-based system that had been created under his leadership.

According to John A. Calhoun, the third commissioner of DYS, by the time he took office in 1976 the community-based model was in trouble. More than 50 bills had been introduced in the Massachusetts legislature calling for the reopening of what Calhoun describes as "Oliver Twist-esque" training schools for kids.

Further evidence that the system was in trouble included the fact that there were some 125 "bindovers" to the adult system, suggesting a lack of confidence in the juvenile system on the part of some judges. A public clamor to lock up more delinquents was also in full voice.

"Our task was to make a system from a movement," Calhoun recalls. Between Miller's initial closing of the training schools and the birth of a new system was the "conceptualization and slow implementation of a real, functioning, community-based system with a remarkably low number of delinquent kids targeted for secure care," he adds. Part of this nuts-and-bolts approach to improving the system involved eliminating some 20 of the community-based programs that had proven to be failures.

Perhaps the greatest accomplishment of Calhoun's term, however, was settling the dispute over secure bed capacity. At the time, the system was under attack for not having enough secure beds. With only 35 high-security slots, critics claimed that serious offenders were not being adequately controlled. To address this highly emotional question, Calhoun convened a task force of experts with highly divergent views on the subject.

After lengthy deliberations, the task force determined that a maximum of 11.2 percent of delinquents committed to DYS needed to be housed in secure facilities. The task force recommended that a maximum of 129 to 168 secure beds be made available for this population, but recommended that a quarter of this total be operated by the Department of Mental Health facilities.[7] Agreeing on this relatively modest need for additional secure capacity reconfirmed Massachusetts' commitment to a community-based system.

THE MASSACHUSETTS SYSTEM TODAY

While refinements such as these were made in the system Miller put in place, by and large the reforms he initiated have thrived and set a standard for other states to meet.

The most distinctive aspect of the Massachusetts juvenile justice system today is that most young people committed to the care of DYS are held in unlocked residential and non-residential programs. There are currently 184 secure treatment beds available in 13 separate facilities ranging in size from a capacity of 7 to 18 residents each.[8] Of the 1,700 youth committed to DYS in 1987–1988, only ten percent were housed in locked facilities.

A recent study published by the National Council on Crime and Delinquency (NCCD) places the percentage of youth in DYS custody who are initially placed in a secure treatment program at the slightly higher figure of 15 percent. Nevertheless, Massachusetts now relies less on secure confinement than any comparable state, the NCCD study observes.[9]

Today, instead of being placed in training schools, most young people undergo a short period of confinement in a secure detention facility or in a shelter-care program prior to a community-based, residential placement. At some point during their commitment, some 80 percent of DYS youth are placed in small, non-secure, community-based residential programs run by private, nonprofit agencies.[10]

After they have completed the residential phase of their program, youths are sent home and enrolled in a variety of non-residential programs. On any given day, about 65 percent of committed youths now reside at home under the supervision of a caseworker and a tracker, who advocate for these young people by helping them with their families, their schools, and their jobs — as well as monitoring them to ensure that they do not slip back into criminal or irresponsible patterns of behavior.[11]

On any given day, approximately 30 percent of the youths committed to DYS are in some kind of residential setting: 400 short- and long-term group home beds, 143 shelter-care beds, and 185 beds in secure facilities. Somewhere around five percent of committed youths are in foster homes.

Very Different from Training Schools

A visitor familiar with juvenile justice facilities in California, accustomed to the 600- to 1500-bed training schools in that state, finds a remarkably different institutional landscape in Massachusetts. It immediately becomes apparent that many problems correctional officials in California and other states face are a result of indiscriminately grouping too many delinquents with very different criminal histories in the same facility.

In the 60- to 70-bed dormitories — common in the large-scale California Youth Authority training schools — discipline is maintained with isolation cells, handcuffs, gas grenades, and riot squads. By contrast, in the smaller Massachusetts facilities, the same type of youth can be handled with intensive staff supervision. In Massachusetts today, there are a number of small-scale programs, ranging from a 15-bed, high-security facility for young men to smaller, residential facilities, to the Roxbury Youthworks non-residential program. A number of these programs are described below.

Westboro

The Westboro Secure Treatment Facility demonstrates how a high-security program for juvenile and youthful offenders can be run in a reasonably humane fashion. A 15-bed program staffed by state employees, Westboro accepts chronic, serious, and violent male offenders from age 13 to 18.

All residents at Westboro have been screened by a DYS panel that has determined that they are appropriate for a high-security treatment program using strict criteria. Judges can recommend a secure placement, but it is up to correctional officials actually to make the placement. This allows them to send only the most dangerous youth to the high-security treatment centers. As a result, unlike many other states where it is judges and not correctional officials who make the placement decisions, all the clients in high security are there for a serious offense or a long history of offenses.

The program at Westboro features individual and group counseling and specialized education programs. A point system allows residents to earn "good time" and various privileges offered as rewards for good behavior. Alcoholics Anonymous and Narcotics Anonymous programs are available. Each resident has his own room.

There is nothing particularly innovative about the Westboro program. The institutional environment, however, appears to be remarkably humane, non-violent, and effective because there are a small number of clients and an enriched staffing pattern (1:4 per shift) that allows the adults to control the facility without being heavy-handed.

When a youth creates a disturbance, staff workers are usually able to separate him from the group and do one-on-one counseling. When the resident calms down, he is allowed to return to the group. Occasionally a resident is sent to his room for 12 to 24 hours, but staff workers claim there are no more than a half-dozen room confinements a month.

In this fashion, acting-out and violence are controlled without lengthy confinement. Clients say that there are only a couple of fights a year in which young men wind up with blackened eyes or a broken nose. The fact that there are so many staff around deters more serious attacks. Because the staff is so firmly in control, clients can desist from playing a lot of the "I'm tougher than you are" prison games so prevalent at larger facilities, and concentrate on their counseling and academic programs.

While the Westboro program is set up for an eight-month period of confinement, some young people stay two years or longer. Every effort, however, is made to keep the period of confinement reasonably short. The theory is that longer periods of confinement can lead to a build-up of resentment and acquisition of patterns of institutional behavior that are dysfunctional for life in society at large.

Prior to release, Westboro residents are counseled by a transition caseworker who sets up a post-release program. While some graduates of Westboro are sent to group homes and less secure community-based programs, 88 percent of them return home on probation with someone assigned to track them and make sure that they are going to school or to work. Residents are released from Westboro on a "grant of conditional liberty," with the clear understanding that they may be returned to secure confinement if they misbehave. In reality, however, only those guilty of serious infractions during their probation are likely to be returned to a residential program.

Littleton Girls House

Even smaller than the secure facility for young men at Westboro is the secure facility for young women located at Littleton. From the outside there is little to distinguish this 200-year-old building as a secure facility. Inside, 12 young women, age 14 to 17, live a highly structured life for anywhere from four months to a year.

Again, what is striking about the program is that young women with long histories of delinquency can focus on rehabilitation skills when they are housed in small groups. The sense of safety and comradeship that can be achieved in a well-run home for 12 delinquents emerges in sharp contrast to the type of institutional warfare that prevails in facilities holding 25 or more.

When they first arrive at Littleton Girls House, new residents are assigned Big Sisters to help them adjust to the program and to encourage them to change their lives. During their stay, girls must attend frequent individual and group counseling sessions as they pass through the ranks from freshman to senior status. Initially, they are tightly controlled and must ask permission before leaving a room; when they reach higher grades they are given greater liberties and responsibilities.

"We don't lock the doors on the girl's room at night. We treat our girls with dignity," explains program director Donna Grisi. There is always someone awake and on duty, however, and the main door of the facility is locked.

Most of the young women who graduate from the program either go on to unlocked group homes, foster homes, farms and ranches, the Job Corps, independent living programs, or they go home with a tracker to monitor their activities.

During the eight years that it has been in operation, some 110 young women have passed through the Littleton Girls Home. Ten Littleton graduates have gone on to serve time in the adult Department of Corrections, while three have returned to secure care within DYS. The rest have been able to avoid reinstitutionalization.

The Grafton Girls House

One step down in terms of security is the Grafton Girls House, an 8-bed, "staff-secure" facility for young women 13 to 17 years old. Here the program lasts three to four months and the front door is unlocked. That does not mean, however, that residents can come and go as they please. All excursions outside the house are supervised.

Most of the residents at Grafton have been convicted of shoplifting, larceny, prostitution, or assault. They live in five bedrooms: two singles and three doubles. Residents are required to do the cooking and cleaning chores and to participate in counseling sessions. On weekends they are taken on supervised trips to the movies or bowling. After they leave the program, most go home with outreach and tracking; others go on to foster homes.

Alliance House

Even smaller than the Grafton Girls House is Alliance House in Reading, which contains six beds for first-time male offenders age 13 to 17. In a house indistinguishable from any other on the street, the young men here, while resentful that they have to put up with a lot of rules and regulations, do not act out in the same way that young men in training schools do. In this residential setting, they behave more like adolescents than inmates.

Run by a nonprofit service provider called the Northeastern Family Institute (NFI), this group home uses peer pressure to change delinquent behavior. "If I walk in a room and a kid has his feet up on the table, I don't ask him to take them off, I ask the other kids in the room why they haven't made him take his feet off the table. We put pressure on the kids and make them the keeper of the rules," explains Peter Downey, program director.

Roxbury Youthworks

Massachusetts contracts with a wide variety of community groups to provide non-residential services for DYS youth. Roxbury Youthworks, operating out of a crowded basement office opposite the Juvenile Court in Roxbury, has won a number of these contracts. Among the services they perform are (1) detention diversion, (2) outreach and tracking, and (3) employment and training.

Ivan Cosme, program supervisor of their detention diversion and outreach and tracking programs says that he and his co-workers act as both advocates and monitors for adjudicated delinquents, helping them at home and at school as well as aiding them in finding recreational opportunities, access to medical care, and jobs.

Some young people they work with come out of DYS secure facilities; others come out of detention programs. In some cases the staff's first visit with a delinquent is while the youth is still locked up. After the youth is released, they keep track of him and make sure that he gets home in the evening at the agreed-upon hour, attends school, and shows up for his Roxbury Youthworks counseling sessions.

Hard Choices

The spectrum of facilities briefly described above — from small secure treatment facilities, to group homes, to non-residential tracking programs — can only work if there is general agreement about who is appropriate for unlocked community programs and who must be confined. Adopting a policy of deinstitutionalization and severely limiting the number of young people in locked facilities in Massachusetts has forced those in charge of the juvenile justice system to make some hard choices.

To begin with, Miller established strict criteria for commitment to secure facilities, to reduce the number of young people entering them. "I only allowed so many kids to be locked up per region. If a region used up all its secure slots and needed more, they had to convince officials in another region to declare one of their kids non-dangerous and release him. This prevented overcrowding," Miller explains.

While the number of youths committed to DYS has diminished from 879 in 1985 to 755 in 1987, the Department now also has responsibility for young people in pre-trial detention. Some observers suggest that the numbers in detention have risen rapidly because judges are

31

using it incorrectly as a sanction, rather than to ensure that arrested youth show up for their court date. The number of youth passing through the state's detention program soared from 3,035 in 1984 to over 4,000 in 1988.[12]

With the number of youth in detention escalating and only 128 detention beds available, DYS administrators are forced to release early some recently committed youth who are backed up in detention awaiting a residential community placement. Among those recently transferred home were the following: (1) a young man arrested for breaking and entering, (2) a probation violator, and (3) a young man who has been in detention for a few weeks for an indecent assault and battery on a child under 14.

The release of the third youth most worries current DYS Commissioner Edward J.Loughran. "He could go out and reoffend tomorrow," he observes. The decision to release him was based on a judgment by staff who came to know him while he was in detention awaiting a bed in a group home. The Commissioner decided that the staff know the young man well enough to risk allowing him to return home — with someone to track and monitor him — until a community-based bed becomes available. It is decisions such as these that have caused a number of judges, law enforcement officials, and legislators to criticize DYS for being a "revolving door" correctional system that sends too many young people back home time and again without imposing adequate sanctions.

Commissioner Loughran acknowledges the problem posed by overloading of detention facilities and a scarcity of community residential placement slots. In this case, even allowing a probation violator to go home was a difficult call, he explains, because the young man had consistently refused to go along with the conditions of his probation. Those who work with probation violators insist that they must be locked up for a couple of weeks to impress on them that they will encounter serious consequences if they misbehave, whereas letting a probation violator out early may convince him that he can defy his DYS caseworker again without risk of serious sanction. Nevertheless, Loughran is committed to resisting the temptation to open more locked facilities.

Pressure for More Secure Facilities

The conventional wisdom is that there will always be pressure for more secure beds. Even before the training schools were closed, when there were some 1,500 secure beds in the state institutions, there were pressures to build more locked facilities, Bakal recalls. These same pressures remained after the training schools were closed and there were only 60 secure beds. It is axiomatic that a system will fill as many secure beds as it allows to be opened, he adds.

Commissioner Loughran agrees: "If I added 100 more secure beds today, they would be filled immediately and there would be a demand for more tomorrow."

In the past, pressure for more secure beds has come from judges, legislators, correctional officials and probation officers who felt public opinion demanded that more criminals be incarcerated for long periods of time.

But in states such as Massachusetts, where a policy of deinstitutionalization has been codified and where the number of secure beds available in the system has been tightly rationed, the pressure to build more secure beds now comes from a different source — the private providers who run unlocked ("staff-secure"), community-based programs and other programmatic alternatives to training schools. These providers feel they need to be able to selectively send their most uncontrollable clients to locked facilities. If they are unable to dispatch these "bad actors" to more secure confinement, then the rest of their charges will realize that their counselors have no real power over them, and the staff will lose control over the residents, they argue.

Miller has little sympathy for staff workers in community-based programs who claim they cannot handle troubled adolescents in an unlocked setting. "I think there should be a highly competitive arrangement with the administrators of community-based group homes whereby DYS officials can say to them that if they can't handle the difficult kids, other providers will be found who can." Otherwise, he suggests, community-based programs will only work with the reasonably well-behaved kids, creating pressure to build more secure facilities for the more disruptive clients.

Bakal, however, claims that pressure from the staff of community-based programs for more secure facilities is healthy, signifying that the staff is being forced to deal with difficult behavior in a community setting where there is some possibility that their charges can learn to control themselves.

But pressure to build more secure facilities should be resisted, because it is only by working with young people in their communities that it is possible to address the real problems that are the root cause of their criminal behavior. This cannot be done in an isolated institution, because it requires confronting the chaotic family life of many of these young people. It requires providing the discipline to get young people to go to school, and help to find a job. The more that correctional resources are devoted to working on these underlying problems, the more success the system will have in de-escalating criminality, Bakal contends.

Finding the right balance between the number of secure and non-secure slots in a juvenile justice system is a constant struggle. Resisting the pressures to proliferate secure facilities requires someone at the top who is convinced of the benefits of deinstitutionalization. The DYS commissioner is in a tough position: on the one hand he does not want to give in to the pressure to build more secure beds that will inevitably end in the re-creation of a custodial system; on the other hand, he has to keep adjudicated delinquents accountable by providing enough locked beds as a credible deterrent to criminal behavior.

Demand for More Unlocked Residential Programs

Not only is there a demand for more secure beds. There is also pressure to open more "staff-secure" (unlocked) residential programs. The pressure comes from caseworkers and trackers who work in non-residential programs, who find themselves assigned delinquents they cannot control.

At one such non-residential program run by a nonprofit group called Compass (Community Providers of Adolescent Services), three caseworkers are responsible for educational outreach and tracking 20 DYS youths. In effect this means that caseworkers oversee adjudicated young people who are sent home under a set of conditions that require them either to be at home, at work, or at school.

One counselor at Compass expressed his frustration that several youths for whom he was responsible were defying him and that there was little he could do about it. "You can bring the kids in and yell at them if they do something wrong, but if they ignore you, what can you do? We just don't have any leverage with these kids any more," he complains. Technically, if a DYS youth defies his tracker he can be sent back to a community-based residential slot. In practice, however, everyone knows that the residential slots are in great demand and only someone who has committed a fairly serious crime will be assigned a residential bed.

"We do not have enough community-based slots at the moment and next year I'm going to try to find the money for 50 more community-based, non-secure, group home beds. That's where the department has been short in terms of dollars," Commissioner Loughran says.

In addition, Loughran wants to open new programs, similar to some in Florida, in which delinquents live at home at night and attend special daycare programs. "If we couple our outreach and tracking with daycare programs, I think it would be a very cost-effective arrangement for some of these kids," he continues.

Shelter Care: Unlocked Detention

The challenge is how to keep young people accountable without the threat of incarceration. Doing away with locked doors forces the staff at residential, community-based facilities to devise inventive techniques to engage the clients, rather than simply caging them, notes Bakal, who is currently the director of Northeastern Family Institute (NFI), the nonprofit group that runs a spectrum of programs for juvenile offenders from its headquarters in Danvers, Massachusetts.

Ten years ago NFI opened Shelter Care in a 100-year-old building, formerly used as a home for mental patients, on the grounds of the Danvers State Hospital in Middleton. Shelter Care was established as an unlocked, short-term detention facility to serve 23 boys age 7 to 17 who are either awaiting a court date or an assignment in the DYS system.

Before Shelter Care opened, correctional experts warned Bakal that it would have to be a locked facility. He defied this advice, however, arguing that the moment he allowed the facility to be locked, the incentive to work creatively with the clients would disappear and it would be run like a jail. "As soon as it is locked there would be two sets of people in jail: the staff and the kids. Before long they would become bored with each other and it would turn into a little totalitarian system." So Bakal created what many believed was a paradox — an unlocked detention program.

Few were surprised that initially Shelter Care was less than an overwhelming success. During its first year of operation, 177 Shelter Care residents escaped, causing its usefulness as a detention facility to be called into question. Ten years later, by 1988, the program had evolved to the point where it went for 350 days without any residents absconding. The number of days without runaway incidents is prominently posted on the wall at the facility and is updated every morning. Residents watch the score mount, knowing that for every 20-day period during which no one runs, they will be rewarded with an off-site trip, entertainment, or popular meal.

Staff workers also try to get new residents involved and invested in the program quickly, because it is usually during the first few days at the facility that clients are tempted to escape. "We make a real effort to see that the new boy has some successes right away, and that he feels good about this place," says Nancy Mongeau, director of Shelter Care. This requires constant effort on behalf of the staff, since residents stay only an average of two to three weeks. There is constant turn-over in the client population; some 700 young people go through the program in the course of a year.

"You have to keep the place interesting in order to keep the kids from running," Bakal explains. "The staff has to learn new ways of influencing the kids. They have to work with the culture constantly. They have to create a positive peer culture and pass it along by making one kid the Big Brother of the new kid."

An Unfinished Agenda

By closing the training schools and limiting the number of locked facilities, Massachusetts has made substantial gains, Bakal feels. "We had to get away from mini-authoritarian facilities that taught our kids a kind of fascist behavior," he observes.

But the evolution of the state's juvenile justice system is not complete and must now shift into a second phase of deinstitutionalization, he continues. "Next we have to involve the families more. Now when a kid is referred to us we go out and involve his whole family. We try to make it into a community affair. In one program we have a group of the mothers of kids meet every week to talk about their kids." In the process the families learn new ways of caring for their children that can help keep them out of trouble.

A lot of fine tuning remains to be done, Bakal insists. For example, he says: "We still don't know how to deal with the families of our kids yet or how to find them jobs." Another criticism of the system is that some of the residential programs have become complacent and that the experience of the client in these programs is not intense enough.

"You have to put the kid in conflict in order for him to grow. You have to face him with his victim if possible, involve him in restitution, involve him with his family, and constantly confront him. You have to be tough on these kids. Some of our programs touch these kids and turn them around, but others don't," Bakal continues.

Assessing the evolution of community-based residential placements in Massachusetts, former commissioner Miller suggests that since he left there has been a tendency to develop too many residential placements for young people who could be served at home. "A lot of these group homes just replicate the institutional ideology on a smaller scale," he complains. "But when I get depressed after visiting some of these places, I just think about what is going on in other states and realize that the community placements are far superior to the training schools and by far the lesser of two evils."

A Wide Spectrum of Options

When he set up the spectrum of alternative programs that replaced the training schools, Miller says, he tried to interest as many nonprofit groups as possible in working with DYS delinquents. "We had 200 to 300 contractors with a wide mix of residential and non-residential programs. There was even a Zen Buddhist Macrobiotic Group Home for awhile. It was understood that 10 to 20 of these efforts would fail and that the programs would be discontinued, but that the rest would make it," Miller recalls.

The idea was to create as wide a spectrum of options as possible, in order to keep the settings small and have the best chance of matching the child to the program that suited him or her. The other advantage of having a long list of contractors was that if a youth failed in one program, he or she could always be moved to another program.

"I told the kids that if a program didn't work for them, they could call us up and we would find something different for them. I didn't care if these kids went through 15 programs in a year as long as they weren't out on the street committing more crimes," Miller adds. As a result of this policy, Miller was accused of allowing the young people committed to DYS to manipulate the system. "I don't mind if they manipulate the hell out of us as long as the kids stay in touch with us and out of trouble," he responds.

A lot of clients fail at one or two programs before they settle down in one that works for them, Miller explains. If you allow big agencies to evolve, when a client fails in the agency he is considered a failure. "I don't see any reason to corner a kid that way," he adds.

In fact, Miller sees the system from a consumer perspective with the adjudicated youth as consumer. "What I'd really like to see is a voucher system where a kid gets to choose what program he wants to be enrolled in." While that is not likely to happen soon, Miller did succeed in making it difficult for subsequent administrations to reverse his policy of deinstitutionalization and reopen the training schools. In part this was accomplished by organizing the community-based providers into a political force that would resist pressure to return to the training school model.

One of Miller's other, less appreciated accomplishments was to move the state's juvenile justice system away from attaching psychoanalytic labels to adolescents. Prior to his tenure, many young people committed to DYS were observed, analyzed, labeled, and then packed away to a training school where they received virtually no treatment for what supposedly ailed them. Miller maintains that he would rather have someone help a young person get a job than have a highly-paid professional attach a label to child who will never get proper treatment.

Promising Numbers

Over the last two decades, the new system of juvenile justice in Massachusetts has performed remarkably well, causing it to be cited by the National Council on Crime and Delinquency (NCCD) as an exemplary system.

A study published by NCCD in November, 1989, tracked 800 youths admitted and released from DYS in 1984–1985.[13] After examining several different measures of recidivism, the study makes the following conclusions:

• *There was "a dramatic decline" in the number of arraignments after DYS intervention. Comparing the number of arraignments 12 months prior to and 12 months after commitment to DYS, the study reveals that among the youth tracked, the number of arraignments decreased by half during the first 12 months and that this decline was sustained during the next 24 months.*

• *Arraignments also declined by half among two subgroups of the sample, those admitted to DYS for violent crimes and chronic offenders with five or more prior arraignments before entry into DYS.*

• *There was a tendency among the youth tracked to commit less serious offenses following their involvement with DYS programs.*

"The large decline in the number of offenses associated with the DYS youth is very encouraging. Even those who continue to reoffend, do so less frequently and engage in less serious law violations over a sustained period of time," the authors observe.

In looking at another measure of recidivism, the authors note that while young people released from Massachusetts training schools in the past were rearraigned at a rate of 66 percent, under the new, community-based system, of all youths who were committed to DYS, approximately 51 percent were arraigned within 12 months of their initial commitment. The study also revealed that Massachusetts has a significantly lower recidivism rate for juveniles than other jurisdictions around the country.

In addition to the NCCD study, while other statistics comparing the old training school system with the new community-based system are sketchy, those crude measures that do exist suggest promising results:

• *It appears that DYS programs have had some success in keeping juvenile delinquents from graduating to the adult correctional system. The number of former DYS commitments currently incarcerated in the Massachusetts adult Department of Corrections has been falling. While 35 percent of adult prisoners had been through DYS facilities in 1972, by 1985 that percentage had dropped to 15 percent.*

• *The number of DYS youth "bound over" from the juvenile to adult system dropped precipitously from 129 young people in 1973 to 15 in 1986. Some claim that this shows that judges are confident about the spectrum of sanctions available through DYS and no longer see the need to send large numbers of the most serious juvenile offenders to adult facilities.*

• *The rearrest rate of young people leaving DYS is considerably lower than the national average. A 1982 departmental study showed that 50 percent of 400 youths committed to DYS were rearrested within a year. Of those rearrested 38 percent were convicted, 16 percent were placed again at DYS, and 5 percent were sent to the adult correctional system. The 50 percent rearrest rate compares favorably with the national average of 86 percent, Loughran observes.*[14]

But there are more than statistics to demonstrate the success of the Massachusetts experiment.

Almost anyone who has visited both a training school and a community-based program — even critics of the new system — generally agrees that the community-based programs are more humane than the training schools. And it is difficult to find objective studies suggesting that public safety has been compromised in the shift to a community-based system. This alone makes Massachusetts a model worthy of replication in states that still rely heavily on outmoded training schools.

[1]Bakal, Yitzhak, *Closing Correctional Institutions,* Lexington Books, D.C. Heath and Company, 1973.

[2]For a description of resident-against-resident violence in training schools see *Bodily Harm: The Pattern of Fear and Violence at the California Youth Authority,* by Steve Lerner, Commonweal, Common Knowledge Press, Bolinas, California, 1986.

[3]Schwartz, Ira M., *(In)justice for Juveniles: Rethinking the Best Interests of the Child,* Lexington Books, Lexington, Massachusetts, 1989, p 6.

[4]Bakal, op cit., p. 157.

[5]Today, the debate continues over whether or not the precipitous closing of Massachusetts training schools was judicious. While the debate may seem academic, in fact it holds important implications for the manner in which change should be effected in other states.

Edward J. Loughran, current commissioner DYS is glad the training schools were closed, but regrets the manner in which it happened. "In hindsight we paid a heavy price in Massachusetts for not having the alternatives in place. It took ten years to really set up alternatives. . . . A lot of kids went into adult prisons because there were no options in the juvenile justice system," he maintains. "The failure to establish enough small high-security facilities for hardcore offenders before closing down the training schools resulted in a considerable erosion of support for DYS from law enforcement, legislative, judicial, and media groups for a number of years," he continues.

"In 1981 when I came to the Department, we had very little secure capacity and the Department was ridiculed for it. We went from 60 secure beds to our current level of 185 to serve the 1700 youth committed to DYS," he adds.

[6]Coates, R.B.; Miller, A.D.; and Ohlin, L.E., *Diversity in a Youth Correctional System: Handling Delinquents in Massachusetts,* Ballinger, Cambridge, Mass., 1978, p. 198.

[7]Commonwealth of Massachusetts Department of Youth Services, "The Issue of Security in a Community-Based System of Juvenile Corrections," Final Report, Task Force on Secure Facilities, L. Scott Harshbarger, Chairman, November, 1977, p. 8.

[8]The Massachusetts Department of Youth Services, 1987–1988, *Annual Report.*

[9]Krisberg, Barry, "Unlocking Juvenile Corrections: Evaluating the Massachusetts Department of Youth Services," National Council on Crime and Delinquency, November, 1989, p. 13.

[10]ibid.

[11]The following statistics about the percentage of youth in different types of DYS programs are drawn from "Juvenile Corrections: The Massachusetts Experience," by Edward J. Loughran in *Reinvesting Youth Resources: A Tale of Three States,* Center for the Study of Youth Policy, School of Social Work, University of Michigan, 1987.

[12]Jacobs, Sally, "Crowding Problems Put Offenders Back on the Streets," *Boston Globe.*

[13]Krisberg, Barry; Austin, James; Steele, Patricia A., "Unlocking Juvenile Corrections: Evaluating the Massachusetts Department of Youth Services," NCCD, November, 1989.

[14]It is worth noting here that rearrest rates are not the best measure of recidivism. Young people who have previously been committed to DYS are known to the police and are more likely than their peers to be picked up by authorities when a crime is committed in their neighborhood regardless of their guilt or innocence. More accurate measures of recidivism are conviction rates and recommitment rates.

Pennsylvania Develops a Wide Variety of Private Sector Programs

Reform of the juvenile justice system in Pennsylvania was prompted by tragedy.

In 1975 a naive, 16-year-old youth named Bobby Nester was sent to the Pennsylvania State Correctional Institution at Camp Hill for a series of petty crimes including possession of a small amount of marijuana. At the time, Camp Hill housed both youthful and adult offenders.

While at the facility for over four months, Nester was subjected to intense sexual pressure by other inmates. On April 2, 1975, he tied his bedsheet to the window frame in his cell and hanged himself. A CBS correspondent on "60 Minutes" interviewed an inmate who reported that Nester had told him earlier on the day of his suicide that three other inmates "were going to jump him." Nester was raped later that day and then hanged himself, the inmate claimed. "Well, he had all kinds of pressure on him — dudes trying to get over on him, have sex with the guy. That's ... that's why he hung up."

The television exposé of Camp Hill in July, 1975, stirred public concern about the violent conditions at the facility. The report and other media coverage also prompted some members of the Pennsylvania state legislature to take a fresh look at their juvenile justice system.

After reviewing the options, the governor of Pennsylvania hired Jerome Miller, reformer of the Massachusetts juvenile justice system, to serve as Commissioner of Youth Services and to create community-based alternatives to Camp Hill. The Federal Law Enforcement Assistance Administration provided start-up funds for new programs, and grants were funneled through the Pennsylvania Commission on Crime and Delinquency.

Four regional offices were established to oversee the deinstitutionalization of Camp Hill inmates. The Center for Community Alternatives

40

was also created to assist in developing programs for the youth formerly in state training schools.

The transition took 18 months, during which Miller had to work out treatment plans and negotiate the individual release of some 400 youths at Camp Hill. It wasn't until January, 1977, that the last 50 youths were transferred out of Camp Hill into these community-based programs.

Since then nonprofit, community-based programs for adjudicated juvenile and youthful offenders have proliferated in Pennsylvania. Institutional placements for delinquents dropped 24 percent from 1981 to 1984, while the number of youth in community-based programs and day treatment programs grew by 20 percent and 50 percent respectively, write Blackmore, Brown and Krisberg in *Juvenile Justice Reform: The Bellwether States*.[1] Similarly, from 1977 to 1986 the number of youth placed in public facilities dropped from 1,846 to 644, while community-based placements increased from 820 to 1,490, they further calculate.

Driving this transformation were financial incentives that made it worthwhile for counties to send their delinquents to the nascent network of private providers. The state passed legislation that reimbursed counties 75 to 90 percent of the cost of any youth they sent to private providers, whereas if a county sent a youth to a state-run facility it would only receive a 50 percent reimbursement. Prior to 1976, counties could send youth to state-run institutions without having to pay anything. As a result, the training schools were packed and the counties saw little incentive to start small county-run programs for delinquent youth.

Today, Pennsylvania's system combines the use of state-run Youth Development Centers and forestry camps with a community-based component run by private providers.

This chapter focuses on the philosophy and treatment methods of three private providers paid to handle some of the state's most serious delinquent offenders. The chapter is divided into three sections: a description of the continuum of programs operated by Alternative Rehabilitative Communities (ARC); a profile of Weaversville, the state's "last resort" program for juveniles, which is run by a for-profit company; and a description of Glen Mills, a large rural institution that has experienced considerable success in establishing a positive peer culture.

ALTERNATIVE REHABILITATIVE COMMUNITIES

Of the twelve programs that opened in 1975 to receive Camp Hill inmates, ARC is one of only two that remain in operation today. Since then, other programs have opened up to replace those that went out of business.

In 1975, when Miller was looking for people to run community-based programs to take delinquents out of Camp Hill, Dan Elby was tending bar in his father's tavern in Harrisburg. A recent

M.A. graduate of Michigan State University, Elby had been unable to find a job on campus in the Dean's Office, where he wanted to do student counseling. Needing a job to tide him over, Elby served drinks and dealt with rowdy customers at his father's bar while he looked for more rewarding work.

When an acquaintance came to the bar and told him that Miller was looking for people to develop programs for delinquents in Harrisburg and elsewhere around the state, Elby hooked up with Robert McKendrick, who became ARC's business manager, sat down at his kitchen table, and wrote a proposal for a residential program to serve 12 kids. Once his proposal was accepted, he rented offices above his father's bar where he did his first staff hiring interviews.

From these humble beginnings, Elby has built a network of small programs and facilities for juvenile offenders, opening a new program every other year. ARC now runs a secure treatment facility for 14 youth in Chambersburg, four staff-secure residential facilities (one for young women), each of which houses 12 clients, a new residential program for male juvenile offenders with mental health problems, a specialized foster care program for 10 youths or more, a day treatment program for 25 youths, and an aftercare program for those graduating from his other facilities. Youths stay in the programs from nine months to three years. The programs handle 100 to 130 young people a year with a staff of 118 and an annual payroll of some $2.1 million.

The early days of the transition from training school to community-based system were difficult, recalls Elby, who is executive director of ARC. Local communities offered considerable resistance to the opening of small programs for youthful offenders. "Everyone was saying that these kids would rape grandmothers and murder little children if we opened programs in their neighborhood," Elby remembers. In one area a community-based facility was burned to the ground; other communities resisted through their zoning boards. In one case, ARC administrators spent three years trying to open a facility in a community that resisted them through the zoning board. Finally, the state supreme court ruled in favor of ARC and the facility was opened.

Despite these obstacles, in 1975 ARC and a number of other community-based programs were established and eventually demonstrated that they could handle chronic youthful offenders at the community level.

"With our expansion we feel very confident that we are able to meet the needs of the juvenile justice system in terms of a continuum of services from security to day-treatment programs," Elby says.

Population Characteristics

Once financial incentives for counties to send their delinquents to private providers were in place, the next question to be addressed was whether the new community-based programs could handle some of the tough kids locked up at Camp Hill.

Most of the private providers quickly demonstrated that they could, but the transition to a community-based system was not without incident. At one community-based program, a youth killed a staff worker — confirming the view of some skeptics who believed delinquents could only be handled in high-security facilities. Despite this incident, Pennsylvania's experiment with community-based programs continued.

According to Elby, ARC has never shrunk from dealing with the state's most difficult youth. ARC accepts almost any youth, regardless of what crime he has committed, and does not evade accepting the "acting-out" adolescent who has an assaultive history and has proven difficult to manage in other facilities.

"Your average mean, nasty kid who wants to take on the whole world is the one we work with best," explains Elby. Soon, word that ARC worked well with aggressive kids began to circulate. "The parole officers heard from the kids that we're strict and that we confront negative behavior. They also learned that after kids had been in our program for a while they began to feel better about themselves," Elby continues.

"We try to stay away from arsonists and youth who have profound mental health problems," Elby says, but ARC clients are not lightweight offenders. Most of them have an extensive history with the juvenile justice system; they have had an average of four prior residential placements before coming to ARC. "We get the chronic, repeat offenders in for assault, auto theft, drug offenses, burglary, sexual misconduct, and those who have gone AWOL from other programs," Elby notes. "Many are sent to us from other programs that couldn't handle them," he adds. The majority are 16 to 18 years old, and for many of them ARC is their last chance before they are certified as adults and sent to prison.

Youthful offenders are placed and released from ARC facilities through the probation department and by court order. Prior to coming to ARC they have to have been adjudicated delinquent in the juvenile court. They are then transferred to ARC either from state-run facilities, detention centers, or from their homes where they have been on probation.

Home-Grown Treatment Techniques

"When they first come to us they are angry about everything," Elby says of the youths in ARC programs. "You can't tell them anything. Most have an assault in their record. Most have been told they are bums. Their self-esteem is shot. Many of them are starved for affection or say they hate everything. It is up to us to turn them around and teach them to take enough pride in themselves so that they won't get themselves arrested in the future."

Elby and others who work at ARC have evolved their own approach to working with these street-hardened delinquents. "We learned how to deal with these kids by experience. When you are new at this kind of work you can be creative. One of our great advantages was that none of us had any experience in juvenile justice. But we came from solid families ourselves and had a sense of what works. . . .I make a point of not hiring people who have worked in other programs. It is harder to retrain people than to train them," Elby observes.

"All my program directors are home-grown. They started out as counselors and worked up through the ranks." The fact that employees see that those who work hard and stay with the program win advancement has kept ARC from losing its best workers. There is a 16 percent annual turnover in staff.

When recruiting good staff workers, Elby has found that formal credentials don't mean that much. "I look for people with heart. If they have heart I can train them," he says. About half of his staff workers have some kind of degree. Staff workers with no credentials start at $12,000 to $14,000; those with a B.A. start at $16,000; those with an M.A. start at $18,000. There is an annual raise based on merit of 5 to 6 percent. ARC is also something of a family business. In addition to his brother, Elby has hired five other relatives, helping to create the atmosphere of an extended family at a number of the programs.

In Safe Programs Treatment Can Happen

When a youth is admitted to an ARC facility, a detailed treatment plan is developed based on the history of the youth's problems and on a social and psychological evaluation. Long- and short-term goals are established. These goals are not just an intellectual exercise. It is a fundamental ARC policy that the staff will not discharge a youth from its facilities until he or she has met these stated goals.

Over time, ARC staff workers have devised methods for working with groups of up to 12 tough teenagers that have proven remarkably effective. The method they use is a combination of "reality therapy" and "positive peer pressure." But what really makes the program work is the combination of the small size of ARC's facilities with a one-to-three staff-student ratio that makes it possible for staff to maintain control of the facilities. Staff workers can enforce a demanding standard of behavior through a combination of staff pressure, peer pressure and a system of rewards and sanctions that holds students accountable for their behavior.

"If kids feel safe and secure in a facility then treatment will happen,"

Elby observes. If they don't feel safe, then progress through counseling and school work is impossible. Discipline at ARC facilities is strict, but it is combined with enough positive attention focused on the students that overall the environment is not punitive.

Behavioral problems in ARC facilities are not given a chance to escalate. If a facility is experiencing problems, Elby, his brother who is in charge of the day-to-day operations of ARC residential facilities, and other members of the administrative staff go there personally to work with the staff until the program is back on the right track. ARC administrators are expected to do more than just sit in their office pushing paper, Elby explains.

Elby's experience in handling drunks in his father's bar and his brother's background as a former Rutgers football player clearly contribute to ARC's ability to deal with youths' acting-out behavior. The presence of staff who can handle physical confrontations gives the students a sense of limits and makes them realize that violent and threatening behavior will not be tolerated.

Significantly, there are no lock-up rooms or physical or chemical restraints at ARC facilities. At most a staff member or sometimes two are assigned to "shadow" a student until he has calmed down. But generally, peer pressure is enough to keep students in line. A positive atmosphere is also maintained by keeping students busy and requiring them to analyze their own behavior and feelings, as well as those of other students, several times a day.

Finally, the residential environment itself is not one that anticipates violence or vandalism. Tables and chairs are not bolted to the floor. The rooms are not stripped of all items that could be used as weapons. One facility has a stained-glass window that staff in other group homes for delinquents predicted would never survive. It is still intact 15 years after the group home was first opened.

Bathrobe and Slippers

One of the techniques that has evolved at ARC is the initiation process. When a youth enters an ARC facility, he must work to gain the trust of the other residents and staff. Symbolic of his initial probationary status in the program is the fact that he is prohibited from wearing street clothes. Instead he is clad in the "stigmatic garb" of pajamas, bathrobe, and slippers.

In the unlocked residential programs, the rationale behind this period of initiation is that without street clothes it will be difficult for a youth to run from a facility. Requiring a youth to prove himself trustworthy in order to become a full-fledged participant also motivates youths to prove that they can be positive members of the ARC community.

45

When a young man or woman enters one of ARC's facilities, he or she is also assigned a Big Brother or Big Sister. During the orientation process, a new resident is not allowed to speak with any resident other than his Big Brother or members of the staff. The Big Brother is expected to serve as a positive role model and help his charge learn how to fit in with the program.

One ARC resident reported that his Big Brother required him to write an essay and do a certain number of push-ups as a punishment for an infraction, but this practice violates ARC policy that prohibits any resident from imposing sanctions on another resident.

The Big Brother system can have a salutary effect on a recently arrived resident, Elby observes. "The Big Brother can convince a new kid faster than we can that it is not worth running away from our program," he continues. Once newcomers have stayed for a month or two, most of them "buy into the program" and can be trusted to go on highly supervised home visits, he adds.

Comparison with Training Schools

It is instructive to compare the experience of a newly arrived resident at a small, community-based program, such as those run by ARC, and the welcome received by a "new boy" at a large, rural training school, where the inmate gangs frequently have more influence on other residents than the training school staff.

At a large California Youth Authority (CYA) training school, for example, the new arrival is typically approached by members of a gang, who test him to see if he is a "fighter" or a "wimp." If he does not stand up to pressure, they will harass or humiliate him, extort goods from him, and periodically beat him up.

If the new resident stands up to pressure and is willing to fight to maintain his dignity, he may be rewarded by being invited to join the gang. A condition of his acceptance by the gang, however, may be to prove his loyalty and courage by beating up or stabbing a member of a rival gang. The incentive for joining is that once he is a full-fledged member of the gang, the youth will be protected by the other members.[2]

The result of this initiation process is that many young people who enter training schools are dragged into a violent gang subculture and are caught fighting either to protect themselves from a gang or because they have joined one. Often, training school residents have their stay in the institution prolonged because of the fights in which they become involved.

Well-run, community-based programs, such as some of those operated by ARC, can frequently avoid this vicious circle because the scale of the facility is small enough that the staff can maintain control.

ARC's CONTINUUM OF PROGRAMS

Chambersburg

ARC's only "secure-treatment unit" can serve up to 14 offenders 15 to 18 years old. Opened in 1984, it is located near a nursing home in Chambersburg, and serves the south-central portion of Pennsylvania. Elby poured $150,000 into the renovation of this aging detention facility and made it about as comfortable and functional as a secure facility can be. There is now always a long waiting list of applicants to the program.

The Chambersburg facility, Elby explains, serves the most dangerous youth in the state. "If our secure program at Chambersburg didn't exist, some of these kids would be certified and sent to adult prisons," he observes. For example, one current resident is a young man who tried to shoot his way into a detention center with a .38 caliber pistol to "liberate" his girlfriend who was detained there.

The average stay at Chambersburg is 9 to 12 months. But when a youth asks how long he will be there, he is told that the staff does not calculate in terms of time. Instead, staff workers adjust the recommended release date in terms of how well a student is meeting his treatment goals. Some students pass through the program more rapidly than others.

Each student receives an individualized Initial Service Plan designed to help him overcome the problems that led to his arrest. The plan sets a number of goals he must work on while in the program. He may be required to improve his self-esteem, his relationship to authority figures, or his problems with substance abuse, family issues, or sexuality.

Life at Chambersburg is highly structured. From the time they get up at 6:30 a.m. until they go to bed at 10 p.m. (1 a.m. on week-ends), students are under constant supervision and are kept busy. In the morning, after wake-up call there are chores, exercise, breakfast, and a goal-focus meeting. Morning educational classes last from 9 a.m. until noon. Following a half-hour lunch break, residents participate in a one-hour group goal-focus session, another hour of classes, an hour of physical education, and an hour of treatment counseling before dinner. After dinner there is a half-hour meeting during which students talk about the goals they are working on, followed by free time until bedtime.

Expectations are clearly spelled out, simple rules are posted on the wall, and negative behavior is confronted both by staff and by peer pressure. "Residents are required to take ownership for what is happening in the house. Everyone is kept accountable," Elby explains.

The strict hierarchy adhered to at ARC is most visible at the dining room table, which accommodates 14 residents. Students are assigned a chair at the table based on how well they are performing at the facility. The student who has made the most progress has the privilege of sitting at the head of the table. This honor allows him first crack at the food as well as having other house privileges, such as being first in line for the shower in the evening and having his choice of which household task he prefers.

After the meal, one student becomes the focus of the group. One at a time, all the other students at the table tell the student what they think of his behavior and how he can improve himself. Ground rules require that the youth who is the subject of this attention keep eye-contact with the person who is talking to him, remain quiet, keep his hands at his sides, and refrain from any form of "feedback" such as smirking, grimacing, grunting, or other forms of non-verbal communication.

In this fashion, under the supervision of staff, positive peer pressure is applied and residents learn to accept criticism. Participating in group meetings several times a day helps students learn to express their feelings. These group sessions also help prevent resentments from building up and exploding into violence.

"Many of these kids have never learned to process their feelings. They have pushed the feelings down and developed a hardened exterior. Many of them have never been permitted to cry or to show emotion. But once you get beneath their tough-guy image, it turns out that most of them don't want to be junior mafia types. What they really want to do is be kids. That's why we have 'feelings groups' with two staff facilitators present who help the students get in touch with their feelings and learn to express them appropriately," Elby says.

"When I Came Here I Was Ready to Fight"

Damon[3] is a resident at ARC's secure facility at Chambersburg, where there are locks on the doors and security mesh on the windows. Were he in California, he would be incarcerated in one of the California Youth Authority's 600- to 1,500-bed training schools. The CYA is filled with young men with criminal histories similar to his.

In fact, Damon is from California, was a member of the notorious Crips gang from Los Angeles, and moved his drug-dealing business to Pennsylvania only after he had been shot in the foot with a 12-gauge shotgun by a rival gang member in L.A.

After the shooting, Damon figured there would be less competition in the East. When he first moved to Harrisburg, the drug-dealing business went well for this tough, self-reliant 17-year-old. Damon thought he had a promising franchise until he was arrested for shooting another drug dealer on the street with a revolver and wounding a young woman passing by. Incarcerated for attempted criminal homicide and committed to ARC's secure facility, Damon is currently working his way through the Chambersburg program.

"When I came here I was ready to fight. Everyone told me that you have to fight in prison and I was ready to hit the first guy who looked at me funny. I had this image that I was a tough guy. But in the groups here the other guys tore all that down until I broke and cried. I found out I was scared and that I kept all my feelings inside and that I didn't know how to ask for help. Now, when I get frustrated and feel like hitting someone, I know I have other options," Damon says.

How much of this rap is just a street-savvy kid learning the new treatment lingo so that he can con his way back to the street as quickly as possible, and how much of it has really sunk in, is anyone's guess. But the fact that Damon is learning to express himself in groups and find new ways of dealing with tension is real.

At one point, staff and students decided that Damon was "shining the program on"—just pretending to change instead of making real progress.

A "crisis group" was called because Damon had violated his contract to change his lifestyle. Crisis groups, intense on-going sessions in which a student's attitudes and behavior are challenged and he is constantly confronted, can last anywhere from a day to a week. Crisis groups can be called if a student goes AWOL, if he attempts to bring drugs or alcohol into the residence, if he is involved in physically acting out, or if he is disrespectful to a peer or staff person.

Damon also had his street clothes taken from him and he was placed "back in the robe." As a punishment for failing to comply with the program, he was given a contract that required he do 60 hours of work during his free time when other students were allowed to relax or enjoy entertainment and recreational trips. His punishment required that he spend 20 hours doing work around the facility, 20 extra hours of school work, and 20 hours talking with peers about some of his problems.

"We get very few incidents where students are involved in antagonistic behavior, fighting with each other and staff," Elby notes. The highly-structured nature of the program and the fact that all students are constantly under staff supervision discourages fighting.

This is not to say that all ARC programs have gone without major incident during its 15 years of operation. Years ago, one ARC student committed suicide. Elby said that the student had suicidal tendencies when he came to the program, but seemed to be making progress. Then, some time between the room checks that come at 20-minute intervals, the student managed to hang himself. Since then Elby has hired the services of a full-time psychologist and a part-time psychiatrist.

Over the last five years, ARC residents have tended to be more emotionally disturbed than those in past years, Elby observes. More of them have a history of drug abuse and have been victims of physical and sexual abuse. Recently, more clients have a tendency to attempt suicide. Dealing with these young people with emotional problems has been a challenge for staff members, who were more accustomed to, and effective at, working with young people who were aggressive and anti-social.

Community-Based Residential Facilities

After graduating from a locked facility such as Chambersburg to an unlocked residential program, a youth continues his schooling within the facility and continues to be involved in intensive group counseling. But, unlike Chambersburg, there are supervised trips outside the staff-secure residential programs and more home visits during which counselors can help a young person learn how to cope with the environment to which he will ultimately return.

The four ARC residential facilities are all deliberately located in middle-class neighborhoods, and an effort is made to keep a low profile in the community. The houses look indistinguishable from others on the block, and there are no signs in front of these group homes announcing that they house delinquents.

Asked why he had chosen to locate in middle-class neighborhoods where community groups often resist the opening of a group home, Elby replies that it is hard enough dealing with behaviorally disturbed young people without the distractions imposed by trying to set up shop in low-income neighborhoods. In middle-class neighborhoods, the focus can be on what is happening inside the house, rather than worrying about what is happening on the street.

At ARC residential programs, students are kept in view of the staff at all times. A student cannot go from one room to another without staff permission and supervision, much less go outside. Residents are not permitted to hang around outside the facility. For recreation they are taken to a neighboring YMCA, bowling, roller-skating, and to the movies.

Often it is assumed that youths in an unlocked group residence can come and go pretty much at will. There is a sense that because there is no lock on the door, the staff cannot possibly be in control of the residents. A visit to ARC residential facilities proves this inaccurate. With a good staff, good structure, and a good program, very tough delinquents can be handled in an unlocked setting.

Rewards and Sanctions

On rare occasions when students do abscond, members of ARC's staff who are on duty at the time are dispatched to bring them back. The time a staff member spends looking for a youth who has run away is unpaid. This policy creates a powerful incentive for the staff to ensure that kids do not escape. As a further incentive to cut the number of AWOL students, the staff of residential facilities that have no runaways are recognized for their good work by rewards, including dinner out on the town and a bonus day off.

To discourage residents from running, when a runaway is apprehended and brought back to the facility, he is surrounded by a "crisis" peer group to discuss why he ran. As a sanction, he is required to wear a bathrobe and slippers instead of street clothes and to sleep on a cot in the hall in view of one of the night staff, instead of in one of the rooms with the other students. This lasts for two to four weeks, until the staff workers feel they can trust him.

Youth who have misbehaved are given a "contract" that requires them to do a certain number of hours of work during their free time. Other sanctions include prohibiting a student from talking with other students, cutting off his telephone privileges, requiring him to study during free-time periods, assigning him the worst chore in the house, or reducing his weekly $5 allowance.

Two residents at ARC programs said they were also periodically forced to stand facing the wall for what seemed to them to be long periods of time. This sanction contravenes ARC policy. "Standing and facing the wall is not one of our forms of discipline. This must have been a case where a few staff workers were overzealous," Elby explains.

Just as there are sanctions, so there are rewards. Home passes, recreation, television, basketball are all part of the reward system, as are trips to the store to buy candy and soda, and a "student of the month" award that includes a public ceremony and other special privileges. Petty as these sanctions and rewards sound, when combined with peer and staff pressure they have a powerful impact on adolescent behavior.

From the student's point of view, the worst punishment is to have his home visits cancelled or to miss out on recreational trips. Recreational trips are not just seen as rewards for good behavior; they are also used as opportunities to teach delinquents how to behave in public. This last year, Elby notes, his staff took 100 students to a baseball game in Baltimore; other trips included camping on the New Jersey shore and deep-sea fishing. ARC also holds its own "Olympics," in which residents from all ARC programs compete in educational and athletic events.

One day an acquaintance suggested to Brian that they would make more money breaking into a house. They broke into a house, encountered a young woman college student, and took turns raping her. "When we left we were laughing about it. We even stole her car," he recalls.

Brian was convicted of rape, burglary, and conspiracy. He served five months in detention, nine months at ARC's secure facility at Chambersburg, and now has to complete 18 months in ARC's sex offender program.

When he entered the Chambersburg secure facility, Brian reports, he spent two-and-a-half months dressed in pajamas and slippers. When he realized he would be in the juvenile justice system for a long time, he started becoming involved with the program. "Once you are in this system it is hard to get out. You have to act right or they set you back. Eventually I had to take a look at myself. Since then I have made some changes." Asked why he participated in the rape, Brian says that he was trying to be accepted by the other young men, who used to make fun of him.

Home Visits

The main thrust of ARC's work with delinquent youth is to reintegrate them back into their home communities. To this end, after a student has been at an ARC residential facility for a month, a counselor is dispatched to his home. The counselor makes the first home visit without the student, to get a sense of the family situation and to tell the parents what to expect on subsequent home visits. After the student has been in the program for three months, a counselor and a staff supervisor or program director accompany him on his first home visit. They spend eight hours on the excursion, dining with the family and walking through the streets of the neighborhood meeting the student's friends. The student is never out of the sight of the counselor and supervisor. After these initial visits, a student can earn two home visits a month, or the visits can be withheld for disciplinary reasons.

Home visits are also used as an opportunity to discuss with the student what he is learning in the ARC program and how it might be applied when he is ultimately released. Seeing the student interact in his home community also allows the counselor to determine whether he should recommend to the probation department that the student be released home, or if it will be necessary to find some intermediate placement.

Aftercare

ARC has five "outreach coordinators," one of whom becomes the student's counselor after he completes his "treatment phase" and enters the "reentry" and "pre-release" phases of the program.

Working out of each of the residential programs, outreach workers oversee students who are gradually being eased back into their communities. During their eight-week reentry phase, students go home from Friday to Sunday and then return to the residential program for the rest of the week. A detailed plan for their return home has been worked out, and they are tutored in employment skills and consumer education. During this period they must complete a "life skills program" with a series of 40 lessons that include exercises on how to put together a resume, solicit references, and interview for jobs. Students are tested on these skills by the staff.

During the last four to six weeks in the program, students graduate to the pre-release phase, where the time a student spends at home every week is gradually increased from three to five days. By the end of this phase, the student is living at home during the week and returning to the facility on the weekends. If the visits do not go well, and a student has violated curfew or otherwise failed to live up to the pre-release contract, he can be brought back to the residential program for a refresher course.

Monitoring Graduates Following Release

Following a student's return home, the outreach coordinator continues to monitor his transition for a period of six to nine weeks. The outreach worker makes home visits to talk with the student about his problems and frustrations, helps him get a new job if he loses one, mediates disputes with his parents, and keeps in touch with his probation officer.

Students in the reentry phase receive a contract that requires them to observe a curfew, stay away from drugs, attend school or a job, and do certain work at home. Those who fail can be brought back to the residential facility for a month or so before getting another chance.

After the pre-release period, the outreach worker stops the home visits but retains contact by telephoning every month for nine months. Students who complete four months at home without incurring additional criminal charges return to the residential facility to take part in a graduation ceremony and receive a diploma. Not infrequently, the judge who sentenced the student, his or her probation officer, parents and friends attend the graduation. The student is then "tracked" for the next two years to see if he stays out of the criminal justice system.

"I tell our students that if they graduate from the program and stay clean and out of the criminal justice system until the age of 21, they can come here and I'll give them a job," Elby says.

Dawn Johnson, outreach coordinator for one of the residential programs, says she usually has a caseload of four youths at a time. Out of 36 youths she has tracked over a two-year period, four (11 percent) have been rearrested. "The ones who get rearrested are the ones who are convinced they are slick and will never be caught," she observes.

THE ARC RECORD

Education

An important factor in the success of youths in the residential program is attention to academics. Each residential facility has its own educational component and every student has an individualized educational program. About 65 percent of the students fall in the "special needs" category. Failure at school was at least partly responsible for many of these young people becoming involved in criminal activity.

The younger students are tutored and referred back to the school system upon release. ARC's education director is responsible for helping a student be accepted back into a school once they return home. The education director helps negotiate what grade they will return to, and in many cases accompanies the student back to school on the first day to ease the transition.

But the public school system is not set up to deal with many of the older, more difficult young people who pass through ARC's program. These students are directed to take a GED high school equivalency exam. Elby states that about 90 percent of ARC students who take the GED pass. Those who don't pass are tutored in the basic skills they will need to survive in the workplace.

"We set up an environment in which kids can learn," Elby boasts. At the Woodlawn residence, 8 of 13 students are working on their GED, while the other 5 hope to return to school. Counseling is worked into the educational program. Discussion and reading sometimes focus on drug and alcohol abuse and sexual conduct. The teacher works closely with the counselors.

68 Percent Success Rate

While recidivism statistics are always slippery, and the numbers game rarely tells the whole story, ARC programs appear to be remarkably successful. Of the students who graduate from ARC programs and are tracked for two years, 68 percent stay out of the criminal justice system. No direct comparison can be made between the recidivism rate of ARC graduates (those who complete the program) and those who leave training schools. Nevertheless, it seems safe to say that ARC's 68 percent success rate compares favorably with the 70 to 80 percent recidivism rate prevalent at some training school systems.[4]

The cost of treatment in ARC facilities is not cheap. If one considers, however, that ARC works with some of the most unmanageable and chronic juvenile and youthful offenders in Pennsylvania, then the costs can be justified. The fact that 70 percent of ARC graduates are not reinstitutionalized over the two-year period they are tracked following release also makes these services cost-effective.

The most expensive ARC program is secure care at Chambersburg, which costs $137.55 a day per student, or about $50,000 a year. Students normally stay for an average of nine months at a cost of $37,000. ARC's four residential programs cost $117.55 a day per student, or approximately $43,000 a year. Day treatment programs cost $60.80 a day per student, or $22,000 a year.

Specialized foster care costs $50.00 per student per day, or $18,000 a year. Outreach services are charged at $14.38 an hour.

Leadership

Community-based programs offering services for juvenile and youthful offenders vary greatly in terms of their quality. A visit over several days to ARC facilities leaves the impression that these are good, solid programs that have a history of functioning safely, efficiently, and compassionately.

Much of the credit for this should be given to Executive Director Dan Elby, who has set the tone for the interaction between staff and students at these facilities. Elby has mastered the difficult art of maintaining discipline without the necessity of a punitive environment.

It is hard to pin down the characteristics that make Elby good at the tough job of rehabilitating delinquent youth. But a few aspects of his make-up are clear. For starters, Elby is serious about the quality of services his programs provide. He exudes a quiet determination and an attention to detail that other administrators often lack. Furthermore, Elby is not a desk man. He likes to get out of the office and visit his programs. From the time ARC was created, he was on the front line, dealing with difficult kids personally. He learned how to handle these adolescents and how to teach others to be firm yet supportive with young people.

Watching Elby move through a facility is an education. While visiting the secure facility at Chambersburg, he tried all the closet doors to make sure none were unlocked. His banter with students and staff showed that he was up-to-date on the issues that concerned them. He can explain in equal detail how a locking system works, how the ARC Olympics are scheduled, and how he won a fight to secure funds for their education program.

A powerful physical presence, Elby does not throw his weight around or use it in a confrontational manner. A former football player and now a runner, he carries himself with a quiet confidence. His manner is also considered and somewhat understated. He is sometimes slow to respond, pausing for time to reflect rather than spitting out any formulaic answers. There is also a warm and funny side to this man, betrayed by a hug for a cook or a passing student, or by a few wry comments that make clear that he sees the comic side of working with youthful offenders.

In summary, one important reason that ARC programs work is that they are led by a man who can reject a youth's negative behavior without rejecting the youth. Elby believes that kids are not by nature criminals, and that if given other options, many of them will reform. But at the same time, he knows that some of the youth he works with will continue their criminal patterns of behavior. A street-smart man, he has learned to be compassionate with youthful offenders without being a pushover.

WEAVERSVILLE:
A FOR-PROFIT PROGRAM FOR YOUTHFUL OFFENDERS

The advantages and disadvantages of permitting for-profit companies to build and administer correctional facilities for juvenile and youthful offenders have been widely debated.

Advocates of private enterprise say they may bring new and more effective methods to the rehabilitation of delinquents. For a number of reasons, for-profit companies can be more cost-effective, the argument continues: they may get better prices from contractors, expand and reduce their workforce rapidly without being restricted by civil service rules, and hire non-union workers.

Critics of for-profit correctional programs, however, worry that, in an effort to increase profits, entrepreneurs will cut corners in providing facilities and services for offenders.

"Private enterprises probably can run prisons cheaper than government," Jerome Miller, former juvenile corrections commissioner in Massachusetts and Pennsylvania, told a reporter from *State Legislature* magazine. "The question is, are they just going to run an outmoded and inhuman system more efficiently, or are they going to bring some real improvements and new ideas?"

Since the mid-1970s a number of private for-profit corporations have offered juvenile justice services in both Pennsylvania and Florida. The pioneer in this area was RCA/GE, which in 1975 opened a secure "intensive treatment unit" facility for "hard-core," chronic youthful offenders in an old psychiatric hospital a few miles from the airport in Weaversville, Pennsylvania. On July 1, 1989, RCA/GE decided to leave the field of corrections. The Weaversville facility is now under the management of the Career Systems Development Corporation.

Located in a rural area amidst cornfields, the Intensive Treatment Unit at Weaversville is used by juvenile court judges and the probation department as a last resort for juvenile offenders. If they fail at Weaversville, they will most likely either be "certified" as adults and sent to state prison, or be locked into a psychiatric hospital.

Weaversville has a capacity to treat 26 males. The age range is from 14 to 20, although most residents are 16 to 17 years old. The average length of stay for residents is ten months.

Some of the most serious youthful offenders from the counties surrounding Allentown end up at Weaversville. Among them are young people who have been found guilty of crimes ranging from aggravated assault, armed robbery, burglary, rape, and arson, to murder. About half of Weaversville's clients have been committed for a violent crime, while the other half are in for drugs or property offenses.

Most residents at Weaversville are serious, repeat offenders. One sample of 47 former residents reveals that the state had previously intervened in the lives of these young people a total of 260 times. Not only have many prior interventions with these youth failed, a number of them have also either been transferred out of other juvenile correctional facilities as "unmanageable" or they have absconded from them.

All Weaversville residents are felons committed to the program by a juvenile court judge or by the probation department. Unlike those run by the state's non-profit providers, the Weaversville facility is owned by the state. Thus Weaversville does not have the option of refusing to accept certain referrals they feel might be disruptive to their program, and only on rare occasions are residents transferred to other state facilities.

While there are other state facilities available for youthful offenders who are either psychotic or who are seriously developmentally delayed, many Weaversville residents are clearly psychologically and emotionally disturbed. For example, one client put poison in his grandmother's milk, stole his father's money, and set his sister on fire, notes Henry J. Gursky, project manager until July, 1989.

Like a College Dorm

First appearances at Weaversville are deceptive. From the outside the Intensive Treatment Unit does not look much different than many other secure facilities for juveniles scattered around the country, save that it is significantly smaller than most. Twelve-foot, razor-ribbon-topped fences surround this two-story brick building, and security mesh covers the windows. For additional security at night, high-intensity lights illuminate the basketball and handball courts and the surrounding grounds.

In contrast, on the inside the facility has an atmosphere more reminiscent of a college dorm than a correctional facility. On the lower floor, students live in two-person carpeted rooms, which they are permitted to decorate with posters and equip with a stereo from home. Each has a key to his room. Upstairs there are well-equipped classrooms, vocational shops, conference rooms, and an indoor recreation area.

On a typical day at Weaversville, a visitor encounters two residents in the vocational training shop. One is learning to solder copper water pipes below a mock-up sink unit as a plumbing exercise. He is receiving individual attention from an instructor. Unlike many other vocational programs available in institutions, this one appears to provide work that is useful and that offers some promise for future employment. The other student is taking a test on what he has learned in a "small engine maintenance" course.

In a classroom, several students are at their desks working on individualized assignments. A number of them have already passed their GED test since coming to the facility and are clearly proud of the accomplishment. One student complains about an essay he must write on how he would handle some real-life situation.

Remarkably, the facility is quiet, clean, and orderly. Overall, there is a sense that the residents are firmly under staff control. The fact that the program is generously staffed with a total of some 26 counselors, teachers, and psychologists—not all on duty at the same time—makes the facility a safe place where the focus can be on schooling, counseling, and therapy rather than on the resident-against-resident violence that is so prevalent in large training schools.

Weaversville's high staff-student ratio makes it possible for students to meet in small groups of three or four with their caseworkers. The facility is so small that the clients receive a lot of individual attention and are forced to face their problems.

"Acting tough doesn't make it in here," says George, a young man adjudicated for attempted murder who sports long hair, with tattoos on his muscled arms. "We aren't allowed to sit around telling war stories about stuff that happened in the street or talking about how great it felt to get high on drugs."

"We don't let these kids run roughshod over the staff," says Henry Gursky, the psychologist who had been director of the program since it opened in October, 1975, until he was replaced by Bill Coyle when the program changed hands in 1989.

RCA's Level System

The chief control mechanisms at Weaversville are a behavior modification system and a token economy. Residents must pass through a five-level system before being eligible to graduate from the program, and the staff must judge them to have made a genuine effort to improve themselves. Interim rewards for good behavior include an allowance and the opportunity to go on off-site trips.

By using the level system the staff requires that residents "earn their way through the program." An RCA description of their level system is roughly as follows:

Level One: *The resident explores obstacles to and resources for "responsible living." Then he must come to an agreement with the staff about the basic issues he has to face during the time he is at Weaversville. He must then agree to work toward appropriate goals in overcoming his problems.*

Level Two: *The youth must formalize a treatment contract with the staff which clearly states what he must accomplish before he graduates.*

Level Three: *For a minimum of three months, the resident must demonstrate that he is making progress toward meeting his agreed-upon goals.*

Level Four: *The resident must demonstrate that he has "internalized" the changes he is attempting to make for at least a month.*

Level Five: *The resident must go through a process of planning for his release that will allow him either to move to a non-secure facility or to be re-integrated back to his home community.*

While many residents say they think the level system and token economy is "Mickey Mouse stuff for kids," none of them sees any way to avoid going along with the program. Fifteen-year-old Anthony, convicted on three counts of burglary and receiving stolen property, has decided to comply with the program because the alternative is worse. "If you don't do what they say they can keep you here for a year and a half instead of nine months. Or they can transfer you to another secure facility that's even worse," he says with the wisdom of a young man who knows his way around the juvenile correctional field. Anthony is famous for running from programs; he has absconded from five so far.

The level system is used to break down the task of treatment into manageable portions that can be monitored and assimilated. Sitting in on case conferences with the staff, it quickly becomes apparent that the staff know the residents, their criminal histories, and their families intimately. Discussion centers around whether a youth deserves to move to the next level, and whether he has been challenged sufficiently to see if he has internalized some of the values he says he is working on.

The level system and token economy, however, cannot always control some residents who are accustomed to getting their way through physical intimidation. Prior to July 1, 1989, when residents acted out and were either a danger to themselves or to others, they were restrained with handcuffs and flex cuffs on the legs for up to six hours. Every twenty minutes an attempt was made to see if they could safely be released from these restraints. Usually only twenty minutes of restraint were required before a resident cooled off, Gursky notes. For lesser misbehavior there is room restraint, where a resident is sent to his room or required to sit in a chair facing the wall.

Room confinement isn't much fun, reports Lenny, a 16-year-old youth convicted of auto theft and assault and battery. Lenny occasionally does something to get himself placed in a room that has been stripped of all furniture save a bare mattress on the floor. "They leave a counselor in the room with you until you chill out," he adds.

Since July 1, 1989, the use of handcuffs within the facility has been discontinued, notes the new director, Bill Coyle.

High Praise

Weaversville has received high praise from both state officials and academics. Robert H. Sobolevitch, formerly director of the state Welfare Department's Bureau of Group Residential Services — responsible for contracting out services for delinquents in the state — is impressed with Weaversville. "It is the best example of a private operation. . . .This is going to be the national model. It's the hottest thing in corrections," he is quoted in the press as saying.

Rutgers University professor of criminal justice James Finckenauer, who has studied programs for delinquents nationwide, also judges Weaversville to be one of the best. "Weaversville is better staffed, organized, and equipped than any program of its size that I know," he is quoted as saying.

One of the aspects of Weaversville that appeals to Finckenauer is that treatment is based on the articulated theory that delinquency is caused by erroneous methods of thinking. Faulty social learning has led to faulty ways of thinking, which in turn has resulted in criminal behavior, according to the theory.

In an effort to rehabilitate the youthful offender, this "faulty way of thinking" is challenged again and again through behavior modification, reality therapy, group and individual counseling. Typically, the violent and aggressive youth who are sent to Weaversville are "lacking a moral value system and guilt feelings about their wrong-doings," writes Finckenauer in *Causal Theory and the Treatment of Juvenile Offenders*. Most of these youth are unable to empathize with their victims, he adds.

To attack these faulty thinking systems and rehabilitate the client, members of the staff pressure their clients to accept responsibility for their actions. In both individual and group sessions, residents are "confronted and pushed" to see if they are learning non-violent ways of dealing with stress. An effort is made to teach a resident how to get what he wants out of life legally.

Therapy at Weaversville, explains staff psychologist Art Eisenbuch, is designed to "hold a mirror up" to these young people and allow them to generate some "self-disgust" for their criminal actions. Only after they have repudiated their former lifestyle can they move on to build up a more socially acceptable pattern of behavior. Behavior modification, using the token economy and enforced on a daily basis by counselors, combined with psychotherapy, does cause a reduction in delinquent values, claims Eisenbuch.

Recidivism Estimates

Finckenauer reports on two internal studies of youth committed to Weaversville. The first looked at a total of 117 clients who had left the facility between 1976 and 1980. Thirteen of these either could not be located or had failed to graduate from the program. Of the remaining 104 former residents, 48 percent had not been rearrested or convicted during at least a year of tracking by their probation officer since their release.

A second internal survey of 31 youth who left Weaversville in 1981 revealed that all but four graduated from the program. Of the remaining 27, 18 (67 percent) had no rearrests within a minimum of six months since their release.

More recently, Gursky reports that a study of 88 Weaversville graduates who have been out of the facility for a period of six months to four years found that about half of them had been rearrested. About 40 percent of his clients go on to do time in state institutions, Gursky estimates.

Is a success rate of about 50 percent good or bad? Finckenauer describes the outcomes as "impressive" for two reasons: First, Weaversville's residents are a difficult-to-treat, hard-core offender population that has failed at other programs. Second, other correctional treatment programs have a dismal track record. Given these two considerations, equipping half the residents with the skills to survive outside of the institutional structure is seen as a remarkable acomplishment.

Cost of the Program

In 1984 it cost $105 per student per day, or $38,325 a year, to keep a resident at Weaversville. This cost, however, must be seen in context. Weaversville is often the last chance for a youth prior to being sent either to state prison or to a mental hospital. A state mental hospital costs the state $300 a day or $110,000 a year per resident. Seen from this perspective, the Weaversville rate looks like a bargain.

Nor did RCA use Weaversville to milk big profits out of the state coffers. Out of a $912,000 annual budget paid by the state, RCA took a profit of only $60,000. Weaversville is able to keep its costs down by hiring staff at wages below those paid at most state institutions. Counselors average $12,000 to $15,000 a year.

State employee unions are not anxious to see Weaversville's non-union operation expand. Unions have proven themselves powerful opponents of for-profit prisons. For example, efforts to replicate the Weaversville model in San Diego failed when the county's union of probation and correctional officers stopped RCA from opening a 100-bed juvenile detention facility. The union won its case by citing a county counsel opinion that state law prohibited private contractors from running public facilities.

While the controversy over whether for-profit companies should be able to operate in the field of juvenile corrections will no doubt continue, Weaversville proves that corporations can run first-class programs and facilities if they put their minds to it. Whether or not the profit motive may eventually cause companies to cut corners at the expense of the client and the state remains to be seen.

However, given the scarcity of good, small, high-security programs for the treatment of youthful offenders, it seems to make sense to offer profit-making entities the opportunity to create such programs as long as they are carefully monitored by the state. If held to strict design regulations — requiring a small-scale, high-quality facility, and a good staff-resident ratio — for-profit programs show great promise for improvement over the outsized training school system that has proven such a failure in many parts of the country.

GLEN MILLS SCHOOL:
THE BEST WAY TO RUN A LARGE REFORMATORY

Not everyone has abandoned arguments in favor of the large, rural training schools and joined the trend toward investing in a network of smaller, community-based programs. Some contend that it was not the large scale or rural location of juvenile correctional facilities that made them violent and unmanageable; instead they fault primitive methods of institutional management.

An effort to reform the training school without abandoning the large-scale facility has taken place at the Glen Mills School in Concordville, Pennsylvania. There, for the last 15 years, an experiment has been in progress that may revolutionize the way large institutions for juvenile offenders are run.

Already, juvenile correctional officials from other states are visiting Glen Mills to see how the staff has established a prep school-like atmosphere at a facility that houses 650 inner-city offenders from 18 states, the District of Columbia, the Federal Bureau of Prisons, and Bermuda.

History

Glen Mills is the oldest reformatory for juveniles still in operation in the country. The third reformatory built in the nation, it opened in 1828 as the House of Refuge of Philadelphia. The best description of Glen Mills, its history and its implications for juvenile justice reform, can be found in *Without Locks and Bars: Reforming Our Reform Schools* by Grant R. Grissom and Wm. L. Dubnov (Praeger, 1989).

Grissom recounts how Glen Mills started in 1828 as a reformatory where agricultural work, schooling, religious instruction, and corporal punishment were used to rehabilitate the inmate.

In the 1960s, military drills gave way to a custody-clinical model. During this period, however, a split developed in the staff, which was easily manipulated by residents. On one side were the "professional" staff of teachers and social workers engaged in rehabilitation; on the other side were line-staff counselors responsible for maintaining discipline among the residents in their cottages.

The professional staff accused the line staff of excessive use of force and isolation cells in maintaining discipline. They claimed that these techniques interfered with the therapeutic thrust of their work with the residents. Told to maintain discipline without relying on brute force or detention, the line staff resorted to making alliances with the toughest inmates in the cottages, granting them certain privileges in return for having them maintain order.

As a result, delinquent, aggressive, and manipulative behavior were rewarded and the strong were permitted to dominate the weak. "In effect the delinquent leaders had free rein of the institution," Grissom writes.

The 1970s at Glen Mills were a period of crisis, when residents were out of control. There were frequent episodes of stronger inmates assaulting weaker ones, many residents escaped, and a general breakdown of discipline occurred. In an effort to regain control, the staff resorted to handcuffs, straitjackets, and an increased use of detention cells.

Transformation

In 1975, with the school $700,000 in debt, the physical plant in serious disrepair, and the number of residents down to 30, the Glen Mills Board of Directors appointed as the new director Cosimo (Sam) Ferrainola, 44, an assistant professor of social work at the University of Pittsburgh.

Between 1975 and 1980, Ferrainola completely transformed Glen Mills. For openers he unlocked the facility, offering a free ride to any of the residents who wanted to leave for reassignment to another correctional facility. Over time, he fired or forced to leave three-quarters of the original staff. He then recruited large, strong, easy-going, street-smart counselors from college and university athletic departments.

Ferrainola is no defender of the status quo at reformatories. "The training school system stinks," he says in his typically blunt manner. "Kids are getting hurt. The government is sending kids to places where they get raped and beat up. Officials send kids to facilities where they would never send their own children. Part of the problem is that in state-run facilities there is no incentive to do a good job. We have an incentive. If we don't do a good job we go bankrupt."

Part of the problem with training schools is that they don't understand the kids they are dealing with, Ferrainola contends. When he took over as director in 1975, Glen Mills could best be described as based on the custodial-treatment model, in which residents were seen as being disturbed as a result of a deprived childhood. A social work approach was used to rehabilitate the residents.

But Ferrainola believed that the treatment model was inappropriate. The delinquents coming to Glen Mills were not "disturbed" and in need of treatment, he argued. Rather he saw them as being part of an impoverished subculture where delinquent behavior was rewarded and membership in a youth gang was a symbol of status. These young men needed not psychological counseling, he believed, but a system that would reward them for pro-social behavior and would offer access to first-rate academic and vocational training programs.

"How can you rehabilitate a kid who has never been habilitated?" Ferrainola asks. "How can you resocialize a kid who has never been socialized? These kids need to be habilitated, not rehabilitated."

"The training school philosophy is all wrong," he continues. "Most training schools treat delinquency as a psychological disease. If you eliminate the kids with severe emotional disturbance from the training schools, what you have left is kids who have adapted their behavior to survive in a very tough ghetto environment. These kids are not abnormal. They want the same things you and I want. They want to survive, they want status, they want material things, and they want to belong to a group," he continues.

Using Peer Pressure to Control the Institution

Following a theory set forth by Howard W. Polsky, Ferrainola believes that the old reformatory model failed because delinquents rather than the staff controlled the cottages.[5] When a youth enters a training school, there is an uneven competition for his allegiance between the staff and delinquent gang leaders. On one side, the staff are trying to win over the resident so he will abide by the institutional rules. On the other side, delinquent peers are exerting pressure on the new boy to join them in defying institutional authority. With rare exceptions, most new residents join the delinquent peer group, because they recognize that their peers hold the real power at the institution and that the ability of the staff to protect them is intermittent at best.

Given this dynamic, Ferrainola felt that the only answer was to collapse the two competing staff and resident cultures into one, and to form a community which imposed a positive peer norm on the resident. To bring about such a change in the institutional culture, the Glen Mills staff was trained to manipulate the peer leadership into establishing a pro-social norm on campus that the residents themselves would subsequently help enforce.

This was not an easy task. An initial breakthrough was achieved when Ferrainola managed to turn a delinquent gang leader from being a negative to a positive force on campus by threatening to send him back to court, where he risked being certified as an adult and sent to adult prison.

To learn how to turn the rest of the peer leadership from positive to negative, the Glen Mills staff was trained to analyze the "force field" in each cottage and to single out the leadership for special attention. Once the leaders were identified, they were offered membership in an exclusive club called "The Bulls," offering them certain benefits in return for providing a positive role model and helping the staff enforce good behavior on campus through a process of respectful confrontation.

Like an invading army, Ferrainola's carefully recruited staff established a positive atmosphere in one cottage and then moved on to conquer the next.

Part of the transformation of Glen Mills required that the staff gain physical control of the campus. Members of the staff physically confronted residents who were bullying, threatening, assaulting, or manipulating other residents. Grissom's research shows clearly that the number of incidents in which a member of the staff hit a resident escalated significantly before the number of resident-against-resident assaults dropped.[6] In other words, the staff became increasingly confrontational with the resident thugs before campus assaults diminished.

Ferrainola supported his staff in taking back physical control of the facility. He told them that they should never hesitate from intervening when one resident was "taking the dignity" of another. He made it clear that he would not tolerate residents bullying, threatening, hitting, or manipulating other residents.

Clearly, taking back physical control of an institution like this can be a tricky business. The danger is that members of the staff will abuse their power. On the other hand, it can be equally dangerous to fail to confront assaultive behavior among the residents. The record at Glen Mills suggests that physical confrontations between students and staff decreased dramatically between 1980 and 1984.

The Positive Peer Culture

Life has changed significantly at Glen Mills since the time when the staff had to retake control of the institution. Keeping the peace at Glen Mills no longer depends on strong-arm tactics. The non-violent norm is so strong at the school that constant surveillance of residents is no longer necessary, as it is at most other training schools. A recent visitor to Glen Mills observed young people walking unescorted around the campus from one activity to another.

A tour of the campus reveals 40- to 70-bed cottages cleaned to Marine-like specifications — the beds made with almost military precision. Rooms that house three or four youths are decorated with posters and photos from home. One of the ways that the administration has encouraged cleanliness in the cottages is by giving each unit a budget for keeping their area clean and allowing them to spend what they save on entertainment or refreshments.

The campus is so peaceful that one is at first fooled into thinking that the population at Glen Mills must be comprised of lightweight offenders. A review of the admissions records, however, proves this not to be the case. Over 40 percent of the population is in for a violent crime. Most of them have been convicted of assault, armed robbery, burglary, auto theft, or a property offense. A few are there for drug-related crimes, forcible rape, or murder. Arsonists, sex offenders, and youth with severe psychological problems are excluded from the program.

"These kids here are tough. They are as tough as any kids at trainings schools in California or anywhere else. We look to accept the worst gang kids from the cities. And a lot of these kids are big. Our defensive line on our football team averages 250 pounds. I don't want any candy-assed kids from the suburbs here. And I don't want any loners. I want the kids who are easily swayed to join the gang," Ferrainola adds.

So how does Glen Mills keep its tough, gang-oriented residents from fighting with each other and with the staff as they do at training schools around the nation? Observing how a recently arrived resident is broken in to the Glen Mills way of behaving is instructive in learning how peer control works.

Guided Group Interaction

Guided Group Interaction (GGI) meetings are held in each cottage right after breakfast. Metal folding chairs are brought out into the center of the commons room and assembled in a circle. In stocking feet, all the students and a counselor sit in the circle quietly with their hands folded in their laps. A student group leader runs the meeting with occasional prompting or guidance from a counselor.

This morning a new student is being told how things work at Glen Mills. One at a time, the other residents have to explain a "norm" to the new student. They start out their explanation with the words "At Glen Mills we always. . . ."

By turn the students tell the newcomer: "At Glen Mills you must always look at and pay attention to the person who is talking to you." "At Glen Mills you can't do any 'non-verbals' such as cutting your eyes away from the person who is speaking to you or smirking at what they say." "At Glen Mills you will be confronted for any negative behavior, but the confrontation will be for your own good." "At Glen Mills whatever is talked about in group sessions like this one has to stay within the group. You don't talk about it to students outside the cottage." And so it continues. Throughout the meeting all the residents in the circle are looking at the new kid who is the object of attention. The kid looks somewhat nonplussed. Obviously, this is not what he expected.

After the newcomer has been introduced to the Glen Mills norms of behavior, the group moves on to a discussion of any problems or feelings that have come up since the last meeting. One resident complains that some of the students are taking too much time in the showers. Another says that people are not being cooperative about sharing the equipment used to keep the cottage clean.

Finally, a young man brings up a personal problem. He reports that his mother is going to be sent to prison and that he is worried that he won't get to see her for a long time. One by one, the other students in the circle give him a positive message and tell him not to let his problem interfere with his behavior at Glen Mills. They tell him that his mother would want him to do well at the school. They tell him to pray and keep in touch with his mother and grandmother.

For an outsider there is something shocking about the group discussion. It all sounds a little too goody-goody. The pro-social propaganda is laid on a bit thickly. One is reminded a little of the Guardian Angels, tough inner-city kids wearing red berets who have become protectors of the public. Everyone is telling everyone to do good. At Glen Mills, the smallest possible sources of contention between residents are explored at length. Proper behavior is described in minute detail. The process for resolving conflict is reinforced again and again.

These young people, about three-quarters of whom are black, are clearly learning a new vocabulary and form of communication. If you listen to discussions between residents at other reformatories, they are the complete opposite of what is happening at Glen Mills. In most training schools, inmates tell each other how to "get over" on the staff. They "school each other down" in the way other residents expect them to act and what to look out for. The art of the masterful put-down is widely practiced. Shouting, rude gestures, foul language, street slang, and threats are normal. Violence is anticipated and in evidence on a daily basis.

In contrast, at Glen Mills the negative peer culture that pervades other reformatories is rooted out with a vengeance. Wherever negativity emerges it is confronted. On those rare occasions when a student does act out physically, several staff workers hold onto the young man until he calms down. Then a staff member "shadows" him until the group is convinced that he can be trusted once again.

For lesser transgressions of the norms, residents are "put in the hot seat," and peer pressure is applied to them to conform to accepted behavior. It is the kind of group pressure one imagines takes place in Chinese communist farm cooperatives. For example, if a resident misbehaves in class, other residents confront him for disgracing their cottage's reputation. Any resident who continues to misbehave is confronted again and again. Most discover that it is easier to conform than to continue to risk rejection by their peer group.

While civil libertarians may be horrified, what works about this approach is that while delinquent young men seem impervious to criticism by any kind of authority, they are very susceptible to criticism by their peers. Thus any institution that can enlist (or manipulate) the residents in enforcing pro-social norms will certainly have a more safe and orderly campus in which learning can take place.

First-rate Facilities

One of the ways Ferrainola is able to keep inner-city delinquents from running from an unlocked facility is to make it a place where kids would want to stay. The school's truancy rate suggests that this effort has been effective. From a high of 160 incidents of truancy in 1982, the school had only 15 cases in 1987. In 1989 the school had gone six months without a student leaving the grounds illegally, and the administration could boast that only one student in 200 ran away.

To make the school so appealing that clients would not want to run, Ferrainola made some very shrewd moves. First he dismissed many members of the "treatment" staff, an action that might not have been expected of a man trained as a social worker. The money he saved was immediately plowed back into improving conditions at the school. The first priority was providing the residents with four good meals a day — including a snack at night of hamburgers, hot dogs, pizza, milk shakes, and other foods that young people enjoy. Students were told that a resident could eat as much as he liked as long as he didn't waste food. For many residents, this was the first time they had access to as much food as they wanted.

The motive behind improving the food was not entirely altruistic. It was hypothesized that improving the quality and quantity of food would make residents less likely to run from the facility and less likely to fight while on campus. "Like lions, adolescents are less restive when fed," the argument held.

But the upgrading of the facility went far beyond improving the food. When a resident arrives at Glen Mills, he is provided with clothes and permitted to select attire from a number of different designs. Students are given medical care and free dental work.

Most impressive are the athletic facilities that are enough to dazzle any public school boy from the city. The athletic program permits the school to field teams in 13 varsity sports, including basketball, baseball, football, track, cross-country, swimming, powerlifting, tennis, golf, and a host of other sports. There are playing fields with bleachers and lights so that games can be played at night. Athletes are equipped with expensive shoes and uniforms. Glen Mills is a member of several athletic leagues and does very well in inter-school competitions. Access to these facilities is seen as a big plus to the residents and is a source of great school pride.

Classrooms at Glen Mills are also well-equipped, with computers, microscopes, and all the accoutrements of a first-rate prep school.

Students may spend their leisure time in a lavishly-equipped student union with pool tables, ping-pong, video games, and a giant TV theatre. The student union is clean, graffiti-free, and patrolled by members of the exclusive Bulls club.

If all of this sounds expensive, consider that the per diem cost of sending a delinquent to Glen Mills has dropped from $121 a day in 1975 to $78 a day in 1988. This was accomplished by removing numerous highly-paid therapists and social workers from the staff. Salaries at Glen Mills are kept low, but there is a generous benefit package for staff members who stay at the school. Per diem costs were also reduced as the school expanded its enrollment. When Ferrainola took over the facility in 1975 it had 30 residents; in 1989 it had 650.

Ferrainola sees no reason that delinquent kids should not be treated as well as rich kids — especially if he can do it spending less than is spent on a resident in a custodial-treatment model facility.

Daily Routine

The day's schedule at Glen Mills is highly structured. Students eat breakfast from 7 to 8 a.m., clean their quarters from 8:30 to 9 a.m., and participate in Guided Group Interaction (GGI) from 9 to 10 a.m. From 10 a.m. to noon they have classes, which are divided into the following study levels: remedial, intermediate, pre-GED, GED, college-prep, or community college. Lunch is from 12 to 1 p.m., after which classes continue from 1 to 3 p.m. Free time or athletics is from 3 to 5 p.m. Dinner starts at 5 p.m.

The evening program, starting at 6 p.m., offers 20 options ranging from access to the gym, chess club, library, tutoring or vocational programs. At 8 p.m. the dining room reopens for hot snacks. A curfew and security check takes place between 9:15 and 9:30 p.m., when each cottage holds a "townhouse" meeting. At the meeting, general information is communicated, students are offered a chance to "own up" to negative behavior they have been involved in during the day, and other conflicts are brought up and resolved. From 10 to 11 p.m. students clean their unit and shower before bed. At 11:15 p.m. the lights are turned out, but students may listen to their own radios or personal television sets (with earphones) until midnight.

Reservations

There are a lot of things to like about Glen Mills. Many Glen Mills residents get their GED, recognize that negative peer pressure was getting them into trouble in their neighborhoods, and have access to first-rate facilities. It is also encouraging that some residents return to Glen Mills after they have been released by the court — and that Glen Mills takes them back free of charge.

But the desirability of continuing to operate programs as large as Glen Mills continues to raise questions. First, Glen Mills has been forced to come up with heroic measures to keep the peace on campus, because the facility is so large in size. Yes, the institution is under control. But this requires a group-enforced rigidity of behavior. Smaller facilities do not need to go to these lengths to establish a positive atmosphere. With fewer residents, even quite a small staff can create positive norms that need not be as rigid as those at Glen Mills.

Ferrainola disagrees and responds: "It has been my experience that when two or more people meet on an ongoing basis that norms must evolve. . . .Normative culture here was put in place when we had less than 120 students. I have learned that once norms are established they are very difficult to change. My point is that the relevancy of the larger/ smaller group is not the primary issue in dealing with normative system change. We have found that the school's normative culture toward pro-social behavior has been strengthened as the population has increased."

While Ferrainola denies the importance of small scale in the treatment of delinquents, it could be argued that a strategy based on small community-based programs is a much more promising way to avoid the mistakes of institutional living that have plagued the field of juvenile justice for decades. In programs where there are 12 residents or fewer, for example, young people may receive enough individual attention to work on their own individual problems rather than on the problems that emerge when large numbers of delinquents are gathered together.

One of the downsides of positive peer pressure in large institutions such as Glen Mills is that the "norms" tend to be very detailed and to quash individuality. Residents are told how they must carry their towel on the way to the swimming pool (in their hand, not around their neck), how they must wear their sneakers (with their feet in them and laced all the way up, not with their heel sticking out), and how they must dress (with their shirt tucked in).

The effect is something like being in the army. There is the "Glen Mills way" of doing everything. Part of the theory behind this is that if you change a delinquent's pattern of behavior you have a chance to change his attitude. But group-enforced norms do not foster the ability of the individual to make choices on his own.

Further, it seems apparent that the positive peer pressure generated at Glen Mills is artificial. Once young people leave the institution, peer pressure will cease to be a factor in their lives. They will not have a dozen peers telling them what is right and what is wrong all the time. How well this model translates to an aftercare phase is questionable.

Were Glen Mills able to release its residents into a network of community-based facilities that could help the residents make the transition to home with more supports, it might have greater success.

Recidivism Rates

How well are Glen Mills graduates doing once they leave the institution compared with those from other facilities? Recidivism rates are notoriously difficult to compare, Grissom notes. However, one study (Goodstein and Sontheimer, 1987) shows that of 527 juveniles committed to ten public and private institutions, Glen Mills' rearrest rate of 51.8 percent a year after release was slightly higher (worse) than the average arrest rate of 47.7 percent.

But Glen Mills did much better when reincarceration data was compared: only 16.7 percent of Glen Mills graduates were reincarcerated 20 months after release, compared with a sample average of 24.1 percent. When compared with reincarceration rates for similar institutionalized populations elsewhere around the country, Glen Mills looks good, Grissom argues: the Glen Mills rate is at least 10 to 35 percent lower than would be expected.

While the merits of the Glen Mills model will continue to be debated, it is safe to say that it is preferable to anything happening at other large training schools around the country. Since it would be naive to expect that all training schools will be abandoned in the near future, administrators at other large, rural training schools could benefit from studying the Glen Mills model. Whether the Glen Mills norm can be easily transferred to other facilities is questionable. It takes a specific kind of leadership and a carefully trained and selected staff to make it work. Positive peer pressure techniques are already being used to good effect in a number of different programs, but they don't work everywhere.

Recently, the use of peer pressure as a control technique was stopped at the Charles H. Hickey, Jr., training school outside Baltimore because the peer pressure had degenerated into threats of violence. Nevertheless, compared with some of the other programs coming into vogue such as boot camps for delinquents, Glen Mills is far superior. Perhaps the strongest point in its favor is that the Glen Mills philosophy recognizes that most delinquents do well when they perceive that they are getting a "good deal." Glen Mills has shown that many delinquents do not need to be "treated"; they need to be given access to resources that will allow them to achieve a successful life through non-criminal activities.

[1] For a brief description of Pennsylvania's transition from a training school system to a largely community-based system see *Juvenile Justice Reform: The Bellwether States* by John Blackmore, Marcia Brown, and Barry Krisberg, Ph.D., Center for Study of Youth Policy, School of Social Work, University of Michigan, 1988.

[2] For a more complete description of negative peer pressure at the CYA see *Bodily Harm: The Pattern of Fear and Violence at the California Youth Authority*, by Steve Lerner, Common Knowledge Press, Commonweal, Bolinas, California 94924, 1986.

[3] The names of all program participants in this monograph have been changed to protect their privacy.

[4] For example, one study shows that 36 months after release, 84.3 percent of young people discharged from California Youth Authority secure institutions are rearrested.

[5] Howard W. Polsky, *Cottage Six: The Social System of Delinquent Boys in Residential Treatment,* New York, John Wiley and Sons, 1962.

[6] Grissom, Grant and Dubnov, Wm. L., *Without Locks and Bars,* Praeger, 1989, Exhibit 1.1, p. 23.

Maryland Shifts Away From Training Schools

Over the last two years Maryland has closed one of its training schools and significantly reduced the population at another. This was made possible by strong political leadership, sustained litigation, and the combined work of several advocacy groups.

Maryland Governor William Donald Schaefer and his new secretary of the Department of Juvenile Services (DJS), Linda D'Amario Rossi, closed the 250-bed Montrose training school in March, 1988.[1] The crumbling, century-old facility had served to incarcerate delinquents since 1922. After it was closed, Montrose was converted into a National Guard training site. The population at Maryland's other training school, the Charles H. Hickey, Jr., campus, has also been significantly reduced.

Closure of Montrose and the commitment to reduce the population at Hickey were only the beginning of an ambitious process of totally revamping the Maryland juvenile justice system. This chapter describes how state officials reduced the training school population and opened a spectrum of alternative programs. It also profiles a range of specific residential and non-residential programs. It concludes with an analysis of the DJS ten-year building plan.

THE SPARKS OF REFORM

The groundwork for shutting down Montrose was laid by a series of critical studies that pointed out glaring deficiencies in the training school. These studies included: (1) a federal report issued by the Department of Health, Education and Welfare in 1967, charging that Maryland over-used institutionalization in its handling of juvenile and youthful

73

offenders; (2) a report by the National Association for the Advancement of Colored People in 1973 claiming that many children in Maryland's juvenile facilities did not belong there; and (3) a report by Maryland's Department of Health and Mental Hygiene in 1986 indicating that at least half the residents at Montrose should be in non-institutional placements.[2]

It took tragedy, however, to hasten change. Two suicides at Montrose caused a media uproar. In one case, a 13-year-old hanged himself from the window of his isolation cell in January, 1986.

Shortly thereafter legal action turned up the pressure to close Montrose. A group of law professors at the University of Maryland filed a class action lawsuit over living conditions at Montrose on behalf of a group of residents in May, 1986. The charges included cruel and unusual punishment, lack of due process, and lack of treatment. Efforts to close Montrose were given an additional boost when the Sierra Club threatened to sue the facility for dumping its sewage illegally. Estimates that it would cost some $12 million to renovate the facility strengthened the argument for closure.

By the time Rossi became director of DJS in 1987, the system was ripe for change. When she took Governor Schaefer on a tour of Montrose, he was so appalled by conditions there that he directed her to find a way to close the training school.

Rather than act solely by administrative fiat, Rossi labored to build a consensus for closing the training school, working closely with the chief judge of the Maryland Court of Appeals and with the state legislature. She also urged key political figures to visit community-based programs in Massachusetts and Utah, where they could see for themselves that an alternative approach could be effective. With strong backing from the governor, Rossi won a vote to close the facility, and within six months the last delinquent was transferred out of Montrose.

Rossi also made sure that the $9 million a year previously spent at Montrose was channeled into community-based programs and services. A state audit of DJS calculates that the agency spent a total of $14.8 million on community-based private providers in fiscal year 1988. With that money, the state placed half of the Montrose residents back home with intensive supervision, family counseling, drug and alcohol counseling, and other forms of support. The other half were placed in group homes, group residences, and other community-based programs.

Shaking Up the System

But there was more to do than simply close Montrose. When she took over as secretary of DJS, Rossi found problems in the way delinquents were being treated at other facilities as well. On one of her first official tours, she visited the Maryland Youth Residence Center in Baltimore.

"I walked into a very ugly, dirty building and a staff worker greeted me with a grunt. I went upstairs and found kids sitting in their underwear and asked why at 9 p.m. at night the young men were undressed. A staff worker explained that if they gave clothes to the residents they ran away." This appeared to Rossi to be less than a sophisticated behavior modification technique.

What she encountered on a tour of Boys' Village, a facility in Prince George's County, was equally depressing. "I went there at 4:30 p.m. and the kids were having dinner, eating at the tables in total silence. I asked a staff worker why they were eating in silence and he said 'If they talk they fight.'" Again the approach was simplistic and did not facilitate the rehabilitation of the residents.

Since her initial tour, Rossi has shaken up the system in Maryland and has required that business be conducted differently. "Our kids are treated better now. They are given more dignity and their value systems have improved," she claims. For example, rather than require residents to sit silently at the dinner table, she insists that the meal time be used as an appropriate opportunity for conversation. "It is possible for our kids to have a positive interaction at the dinner table and they need to experience that," she insists.

Backing the System Down

In addition to changing the way counselors work with DJS delinquents, Rossi's main accomplishment has been to close institutional beds and open up community-based residential and non-residential programs. "When I came here we had a very small number of residential beds in the community. So what we did was we bumped kids backwards through the system. We moved kids from institutions (Montrose and Hickey) to community-based residential programs; others from group homes to non-residential programs; and some kids in non-residential programs we moved out of the system entirely." As a result, the average daily population in Maryland's training schools has declined by two-thirds over the last five years.[3]

Average Daily Population in Maryland Training Schools

FY 1985	FY 1986	FY 1987	FY 1988	FY 1989	FY 1990
728	595	542	379	233	206

While statistics on the growth of the DJS community-based programs are sketchy, the number of budgeted, community-based, residential beds increased from 689 beds in FY 1986 to 932 beds in FY 1989. These figures, however, do not include young people in DJS community-based residential programs that were paid for by other state agencies. The total average daily population in community-based residential programs at DJS in FY 1989 was 1,029.

As the population has shifted from training schools to community-based programs and in-home services, the apportionment of the budget has also shifted. The percentage of DJS's budget devoted to training schools has diminished from 64 percent to 47 percent, while the community-based programs' share of the budget has risen from 36 percent to 53 percent.

Political Battle

The political battle to close Montrose and to reduce the population at Hickey has been hard-fought. Rossi's relationship with some of the staff workers at Hickey has been particularly bruising. There are several reasons for this. First, by reducing the population at Hickey, Rossi no doubt caused the staff to fear that the facility would eventually be closed as Montrose had been, and that they risked losing their jobs. Second, Rossi required changes in the treatment of residents at Hickey that some staff resented. For example, she required that the staff reduce the administration of psychotropic drugs to disturbed residents. She also imposed curbs on the use of isolation cells as a control mechanism. It has even been suggested that some staff workers tried to embarrass Rossi politically and subvert her reform initiative by allowing residents at Hickey to escape and to cause campus disturbances.

The union that represents DJS workers at Hickey "tried to sabotage my political support" for reducing the training school population and changing the way the facility was run, Rossi contends. Union officials spread stories among Maryland legislators that young people committed to DJS were inadequately supervised and were out on the streets "maiming people," she continues. Rossi maintains that these tactics failed because she enjoyed strong support from the governor and five key legislators.

Have the hard-fought changes made in the Maryland juvenile justice system paid off? Of some 12,000 juveniles under supervision by the agency, 85 percent now are supervised in non-residential programs and probation services while they live at home. Only 6 percent are incarcerated in institutions, while the remainder are served in small, community-based residential programs.

A SPECTRUM OF SERVICES

Deinstitutionalization has been facilitated in Maryland by two major accomplishments: articulation of well-crafted commitment criteria that encourage community-based planning and discourage inappropriate institutionalization, and creation of a wide spectrum of placement and service options.

The state's range of services for treating troubled youth is impressive. The first level of alternatives to institutionalization consists of prevention and diversion programs to keep young people out of the criminal justice system who can be handled with other services.

The next level of options is called "non-residential alternatives." These include probation, daycare programs, counseling services, educational services, and community service, in which adjudicated delinquents are required to do unpaid work in the community after school hours. Examples of tasks they perform include picking up trash, cutting wood for the elderly, painting, and custodial work.

Other non-residential alternatives include "intensive supervision" and "electronic monitoring." Intensive supervision means that a young person convicted of a crime may serve his sentence at home, but he must meet with his counselor either daily or weekly as required. He may also be under contract to participate in drug or alcohol counseling or family counseling. Intensive supervision is sometimes backed up with modern technological hardware that facilitates daily surveillance of delinquents who serve their term at home. Juveniles under surveillance must wear a special, non-removable electronic bracelet at all times. Random computerized telephone calls are made to the young man's home, and he can show that he is there by plugging the bracelet into a device on the phone. Thus the monitor can determine whether the youth is abiding by his contract.

For offenders who require a higher level of supervision, a variety of residential programs are available. These include:

• "Shelter care," for young people undergoing diagnostic evaluation or awaiting a court appearance;

• Two levels of foster care: Level I, in which juveniles are placed in a home with up to four young people, and are supervised by trained but non-salaried foster parents; and Level II, in which they live with salaried foster parents and have access to the services of social workers, addiction services, and other specialized support services;

• Two levels of group homes: Level I, which includes 5- to 12-bed residences with 24-hour supervision; and Level II group homes, which provide closer supervision and more intensive counseling than the first;

• "Specialized treatment centers" that offer a trained clinical staff, for young people committed to DJS who are physically or emotionally handicapped, addicted, retarded, or emotionally disturbed;

• "Alternative living units" in which up to three youths live in an apartment or private home where they are helped with their adjustment to the community;

• "Independent living units" where older youths live together in apartments under minimal supervision, with an emphasis on teaching job skills, basic living skills, budgeting and family planning;

• Institutional care in a large, state-run facility is reserved for young people who require secure confinement, those who are a danger to themselves or to others, those charged with violent crimes, or those who have not responded well in community programs.

This spectrum of placement options offers Maryland correctional officials considerable flexibility in prescribing treatment for adjudicated delinquents. It also allows them to spend money more efficaciously by matching the individual needs of a delinquent with a specific package of services.

National Center on Institutions and Alternatives Plays a Key Role in Reducing Maryland's Institutionalized Population

Closing Montrose and reducing the population at Hickey (Maryland's other training school) would have been considerably more difficult were it not for an established group of experts who make a profession of finding and creating community-based placements for previously institutionalized young people.

David Tracey's job is to create individualized community-based alternatives for young people incarcerated in training schools. A ten-year veteran of the Alexandria, Virginia-based National Center on Institutions and Alternatives (NCIA), Tracey was, until recently, program director of the Maryland Juvenile Advocacy Program.[4] His office was in the heart of the Charles H. Hickey, Jr., training school, a sprawling 600-acre campus outside of Baltimore.

For the last two years, NCIA has held a contract with DJS to help close Montrose and reduce the population at Hickey. A team of seven NCIA staffers formulated individual treatment plans for 117 residents at the Montrose training school, and relocated them all over a period of six months.[5] Off-campus placements have also been found for 75 Hickey residents.

NCIA's role in Maryland includes working with DJS staff to develop a broad network of private providers. Every month Tracey receives a "vendor list" of private providers who are willing to accept DJS delinquents into their program. The list includes a brief description of the program, the program's capacity for male and female residents, the number of vacancies, the number of residents who have run away from the facility, and the number of DJS youth already in the program.

"The more you individualize the treatment, the better your chances are of reaching a kid and making a difference," Tracey argues. Nationwide, NCIA staff workers have developed some 7,000 plans that offer alternatives for institution-bound people. About 70 percent of the plans have been accepted by the authorities and put into effect.

Generally NCIA recommends programs that emphasize supervision of the youth in his community, rather than isolation in a locked facility.

However, some of NCIA's treatment plans include a period of "down time" in a locked facility. For example, NCIA recommended six months in a locked facility followed by six months in a residential staff-secure facility, followed by victim restitution for one young man, convicted of rape, who had already served some confinement time. Tracey emphasizes though, that if a youth is sentenced to serve time in a small locked facility, it should be for a limited period, after which he should move into a community-based program.

Consumer Perspective

A key factor in making the community-based system work is allowing youths to participate in decisions about their own placement, Tracey continues.

"We try to have a consumer perspective," he explains. That means that in developing alternative treatment plans for each resident, the youth is allowed some say in what kind of community placement he thinks would work best for him.

"Research shows that the more you let kids invest in their own decision-making, the stronger the chance you have to make it work," Tracey notes. "This does not imply that because a youth says he will go along with a placement it will succeed," he warns. "It does, however, allow a counselor to instill a sense of personal responsibility in the youth whose placement is not working out by saying: 'Wait a minute, this was your idea, not mine.'"

Frequently, young people who are transferred out of training schools into community-based programs defy the rules, or run from a group home. It is important to use such a crisis as an opportunity to intervene and change the youth's behavior, Tracey maintains. If the state's immediate response is to send the youth back to the training school, then nothing is gained, he argues. The goal is not simply to move youths out of the schools. Rather, it is to make non-residential placements successful.

"Adolescence is not an event; it is a process," he adds. "Some youth go through ten placements before they realize that they have to take some responsibility for their lives.

"I tell the kid, 'Look, if this isn't working we will find something that will work. What we are about is keeping you out of an institution. We try to make the program fit the kid, and not the kid fit the program,'" he adds.

Sending Hoods to the Woods

Developing alternatives to incarceration in large state training schools does not necessarily mean that a delinquent should return to his community of origin, Tracey observes. Most youths do return to their home community, and the best one can do is to offer them supports to help deal with their environment productively. "But for some kids, returning to their neighborhood means instantaneous non-survival," he notes.

One approach that has been used with some success is placing delinquents in wilderness programs, an approach sometimes referred to as sending "hoods to the woods." Benefits that can flow from placing the youth in an unfamiliar, challenging environment include an increase in the delinquent's sense of self-esteem and assertiveness, qualities that can help a delinquent resist some of the negative peer pressure he may encounter when he eventually returns home.

"I think these programs can work," Tracey asserts. It can serve as a kind of rite of passage for a young man, not unlike a tour of duty in the army. Maryland sends young people to a number of these wilderness programs, including Outward Bound and Vision Quest.

Status Reports

Every month Tracey provides DJS with a status report on all NCIA transfers that is compiled from an 18-item questionnaire. This report provides state youth corrections administrators with a snapshot of how the youth and the various community-based programs are performing.

To prepare the status report, NCIA staff workers call the person who has the most significant role in the delinquent's life — a family member, foster parent, probation officer, or counselor at a residential program. Among the questions asked are whether the youth has been going to school, whether he is sticking with the conditions of his contract, and whether there has been any residential movement or a crisis, such as rearrest. Often, the information can be confirmed by a second source for accuracy.

EXAMPLES OF MARYLAND'S ALTERNATIVE PROGRAMS

The following sections describe some of the community-based programs developed as part of Maryland's deinstitutionalization effort.

The Martin Pollak Project

Barry has personal experience of Maryland's transition from a training school to a community-based juvenile justice system. At 17, this six-foot-two-inch, 325-pound young man has passed through both the Montrose and Charles Hickey, Jr., training schools. Since being released from Hickey, he has lived at a group home run by the Martin Pollak Project in Saverna Park, Maryland.

80

Barry's journey through Maryland's training schools is instructive. As a young adolescent, he was arrested for giving false information to a 911 emergency operator and for trespassing. These offenses launched him on a journey through Maryland's juvenile justice system. For making false emergency calls, Barry spent 10 months at Montrose. Subsequently, after twice violating the terms of his probation, he was returned to Montrose for another 8 months. It was during this period that he started becoming involved in fights.

"At that time I was smaller so people beat up on me," he explains. "I got banked (assaulted) by a bunch of kids and they broke my arm," he adds.

After a series of gang fights, Barry was transferred from Montrose to Hickey, where the older, larger, tougher kids were incarcerated. Barry spent a year at Hickey.

Fortunately for Barry, Maryland JSA administrators were determined to reduce the number of juveniles in training schools and he was transferred to a small, nonprofit, community-based group home run by the Martin Pollak Project. It has taken Barry some time to adjust to his new circumstances. No longer surrounded by large groups of delinquent youth, Barry no longer has to act tough in order to defend himself. But his impulsive behavior has not vanished overnight.

Barry says he still loses his temper, and for a guy of his size that can be scary. Fortunately, when he does act out, Barry takes out his frustration on inanimate objects. Recently he destroyed a wall in the six-bed group home where he has lived for the last year. "They made me fix the wall," he recounts.

Instead of being locked up with hundreds of other delinquents on a regimented campus behind razor-wire fences, Barry is out in the community under strict supervision, working in a job with a group called the "A Team," where he does carpentry and masonry work. His chief complaint is that life at the group home is boring, but one gets the sense that Barry is at the stage where he would have said the same thing if one had visited him at home or at school. The counselors fault him for spending too much time sleeping and watching television. "They are always nagging at me to do something," he says with exasperation.

Running away from the group home, however, is not an attractive option, because once caught he would just be placed in a stricter program, he explains. "I want to get out of this system so I have to be cool." The counselors at the group home have impressed him with at least one axiom to live by: "First you do what you have to do, before you can do what you want to do."

Barry's ambitions seem wildly out of sync with his current abilities, but at least his imagination seems to have been set free. He wants to go home and become a laser technician. Unfortunately, there isn't much of a home for Barry to return to. For years prior to his incarceration in Montrose and Hickey he bounced back and forth between two apartments, one occupied by his aunt and the other by his uncle.

"He is one of these kids who has just floated for a long time without any consistency in his life," explains Sandy Smolnicky Stern, executive director at Martin Pollak. "We try to keep some of these kids long enough to give them a sense of continuity," she adds. But DJS wants to move them back home as quickly as possible, so a negotiation takes place. As soon as Barry has had some good home visits with his aunt, he will be allowed to move in with her, she says.

Unconditional Care

The guiding philosophy of those who work at the Martin Pollak Project (MPP) is "unconditional care." What this means is that counselors and administrators at MPP will care for anyone accepted into their program "no matter what they do." Sometimes this means bailing kids out of jail or advocating for them not to be charged when they get into trouble, Stern notes.

As an example of this policy, Stern cites the case of Wendy, a girl of 14 who came to MPP on charges of prostitution and drug use. During her four and one-half years at MPP, Wendy bore two children and generally ran the staff ragged. She went through every foster home and group home in the agency. Many other programs would have given up on her, perhaps dispatching her to a mental hospital and her kids to foster homes.

Determined not to let this impulsive and unmanageable young woman slide even deeper into an institutionalized life, Stern says, they finally decided to set her up in her own apartment with a live-in advocate who counseled her and made sure her children were unharmed. The annual cost of the program was $67,000.

To keep Wendy from acting irresponsibly, her counselor used behavior modification techniques. Wendy was paid $100 a week allowance. If she failed to show up for a therapy session, her counselor would charge her for it and deduct money from her allowance. This intensive program seems to have worked, and Wendy is sticking to it. In the process, a family has been kept intact, a young woman has been helped to live a quasi-normal, semi-independent life, and the state has been saved a lot of money. All in all, it is counted a success.

A Variety of Programs

Martin Pollak offers the DJS a range of programs:

• **Foster Homes.** MPP operates foster homes, mostly in Baltimore, for

50 young people admitted from JSA and from Maryland's Department of Social Services. MPP counselors recruit and train foster parents and accompany them to the first meeting with the young person who will live in their home. MPP provides foster parents with a "difficulty of care" tax-free payment, a $15 per day room-and-board payment, and a clothes allowance for the youth in their care.

"We see the foster parent as part of our team," Stern says. They are asked to keep a notebook of observations about their foster child, but it remains up to the MPP staff to make clinical decisions, such as what the consequences should be for misbehavior. A case manager visits the foster home weekly for consultation.

• **Group Homes.** MPP also runs two group homes, one that houses five young men, the other for five young women. The homes are designed for some of the more disturbed young people, who are unable to live in a family setting without acting out. Group home staff members work an eight-hour shift.

The group homes also serve as a more controlled environment into which Martin Pollak administrators can transfer young men or young women who prove too difficult to live in foster homes. MPP also continues to receive transfers to their group homes from the Charles H. Hickey, Jr., training school.

• **Independent Living.** Older adolescents who have been through MPP's program, and for whom there are no other options, can graduate to "independent living." Counselors are assigned to help them make decisions about housing, education, and career choices. There are currently two young people in this program.

• **Home-Based Program.** MPP also uses a team approach to supervise young people who are returned to their homes. Members of the three-person professional team are a youth advocate, who visits the young person at home 20 hours a week, and a case manager and a therapist, who each make home visits at least once a week. "Often our team ends up counseling the whole family and not just the individual adolescent," Stern observes.

Difficulty at the Beginning

By and large the transition to a community-based system in Maryland has been a success, Stern notes. However the process can hardly be described as flawless. When DJS first started transferring young people out of Montrose, there was a rush to open up new programs, she continues.

Her chief criticism is that many Maryland providers already running programs for youth were unable to build new programs because there was no start-up money to hire a staff and open a facility. DJS would only pay for programs after the first resident had arrived.

"This made the provider community look unresponsive, because most did not have enough money to start a new program," Stern observes. As a result, a number of large, out-of-state providers came in and set up programs. Stern also feels that DJS should have done more in the way of producing literature and videos to help private providers educate their community about the need to open community-based programs.

Despite the difficulty in starting up programs, Stern says that the young people transferred from Montrose and Hickey to MPP programs have done well. "What we found was that those kids who had been in the training schools the longest were the hardest to work with. But we were successful with a number of them," she concludes.

Thomas O'Farrell Youth Center

"This place is like the Holiday Inn compared with Hickey. At Hickey you had to be fast with your hands." recalls Jerome, a 16-year-old, six-foot-four-inch, 210-pound drug dealer from Washington, D.C. The "Holiday Inn" Jerome is describing is in fact the Thomas O'Farrell Youth Center, a 40-bed, rural, staff-secure program located off a lonely back road in Woodstock, Maryland.

Jerome has been at O'Farrell for ten months and is impressed with the program. "When I came here I was hard-headed, cussing the staff, fighting, and making trouble. At first I couldn't deal with authority. They would tell me to do something and I would just 'go off'. They used to have to get some big men to hold me down."

But the staff convinced Jerome that he was a natural leader, and they turned him from playing a negative to a positive role. "What I like about this place is that you get to sit back and talk about your life and your history. The staff 'gets down' with you here. They know you real well. They know all about your mother, your sister, your girl friend, and what scares you. Now I'm doing good here. I'm a senior resident— almost like a junior member of the staff."

Sitting on a bench in the sun adjacent to a pathway between the residents' living quarters and the administrative building, Jerome seems relaxed and reflective about his life. He describes the year-and-a-half he spent in a training school in Georgia for an armed robbery he pulled with a .357 magnum revolver. He talks about life on the streets of Washington, where he claims he used to make two to three thousand dollars a day in the drug trade—probably a gross exaggeration.

"But you know," he confides, "there are people who can make that much money without breaking the law."

When it comes to future plans, Jerome is a little vague. He is very clear, however, about not wanting to return to jail. "I wasted too much time already sleeping in dormitories and being told what to do every

84

minute," he says. A good basketball player, Jerome has considered trying to become a professional athlete. But he says he is more drawn to trying to help other young people like himself who have been in trouble with the law.

Asked about security around the facility, Jerome laughs. "Where you going to run to?" he asks. "You try to take off through the woods you will probably meet up with all kinds of wild animals or a farmer with a shotgun." The only residents he knows of who tried to run from the Center were recaptured rapidly by the state police.

Asked whether there is fighting on the campus between residents, Jerome says it is not like that here, but that some residents are fearful when they first arrive. Jerome points to a small, frail 13-year-old, who was so terrified that he hid in the false ceiling of the living quarters on one of his first nights and then tried to run away. Since then, the boy has realized that no one is going to hurt him and that he is safe at O'Farrell.

In fact O'Farrell does appear to be safe. The youth are kept busy and engaged in various educational, recreational, and counseling activities. During a recent visit, the program was in a "shut-down" mode because the residents had not been "respecting the program"—in other words, behavior had become too loose. As a result, the weekend excursion and other privileges had been suspended until the residents proved they were willing to go along with the program.

But the campus has not always been so peaceful, notes Ronald Kerry, O'Farrell's assistant director. Prior to Northeastern Family Institute taking over the facility in October, 1988, it was run by another nonprofit organization. Under the previous administration, counselors allegedly did not have control over the facility, Kerry notes, and a boy was badly injured when other residents did damage to his internal organs with a broomstick.

Since NFI has taken over, there have been no major incidents, Kerry continues. Currently 35 of the 40 beds are filled with clients, ages 13 to 18, who spend about six to nine months at O'Farrell. Most of those accepted into the program are property offenders, young people charged with substance abuse, and a few convicted of assault. Classes, recreation, and counseling all take place on campus; and those young people who abide by the rules of the program are taken on weekend off-campus excursions.

Jerome sums up the system succinctly: "Here, it's perk for perk. If you give something you get something."

Aftercare

NCIA has a contract to provide aftercare, tracking, and monitoring services with O'Farrell's parent company, NFI. Since February, 1989,

Melanie Hoelter has been developing and implementing community-based aftercare plans for O'Farrell residents. She helps O'Farrell graduates find a place to live, a place to go to school, substance abuse treatment programs, Big Brother advocates, and recreational opportunities; as well as helping with resume-writing, securing job interviews, and a host of other services.

The program's clinical staff has identified six residents who are likely to leave the facility in the near future, and Hoelter concentrates on working with them on their release plan. For a one-year period following their release from O'Farrell, she tracks and monitors their progress by telephone. She stays in communication with the former residents, their probation officers, their parents, and their schools or employers. Of the 18 graduates she has worked with so far, 16 are doing well and two have been rearrested on narcotics charges.

Non-Residential Programs:
Fort Smallwood Park Marine Institute

Non-residential programs have also been useful in the de-institutionalization of young people who were previously locked up at Hickey. Staff workers at one of these day programs, the Fort Smallwood Park Marine Institute (FSMI) on Chesapeake Bay, go to Hickey to interview residents before enrolling them.

"Hickey kids are tougher to work with than others," observes FSMI executive director David Paltrineri. "The longer they have been at the training school, the more they act like educated criminals." Furthermore, a lot of Hickey graduates are under the impression that they have "done their time," and resent being told that now they will have to spend their days at a non-residential program.

Nevertheless, a number of Hickey veterans do participate in the FSMI program, which runs five days a week from 8:30 a.m. to 3:30 p.m. There, at a cost to the state of $36.50 a day, they are provided with an academic program that raises grade level by an average of two years over a six-month period.

In addition to classroom studies, at FSMI young people also learn skills that will assist them in finding jobs after their education is completed. In order to gain promotion from one rank to the next, students must make a presentation before two staff workers in which they "sell themselves" by arguing that the work they have done and their behavioral record are deserving of reward. Just as they would for a job interview, students must dress in a jacket and tie, shake hands, and keep eye contact while making their case by presenting their attendance record, class completion cards, and cooperation charts.

Those who do well in the program are rewarded with "points"

accumulated. By accumulating points in a "bank account," they can bid to participate in river tubing excursion to West Virginia, or to purchase items such as a record album or T-shirt. Students can participate in once-a-month overnight trips and twice-a-month daytrips, in addition to frequent boating, swimming, fishing, and scuba diving.

Additional Non-Residential Services

Many of the NCIA alternatives to training schools involve matching delinquents with "mentors," "proctors," "youth advocates," "Big Brothers," or "shadows." These are people who are paid to keep track of the delinquent, interact with him or her, provide some counseling and give structure to their lives. For example, if a delinquent continues acting up while he is at school, then a college-aged student may be hired to go to school with him and help him adjust. Compared with the expense of institutionalizing a young person, these tracking, monitoring, and counseling services can be very cost-effective.

"You can put these kids in the 'goon garage' (psychiatric hospital) for $120,000 a year, or you can pay someone, or a community-trained team, to work with them and interact with them on a daily basis in their community," Tracey comments.

Not all community-based alternatives to institutionalization are cheap. An example of this is the case of a 13-year-old, previously committed to Montrose, who had been diagnosed as psychotic, behavior-disordered, and having drug and alcohol problems. At Montrose the boy had been completely out of control and assaultive. To move him out of the facility required a specialized foster home, supported with services provided by a therapist who saw him every day, as well as an educational specialist. The cost of this enriched program was $110,000 for the first year. This expense was reduced in subsequent years as various services were dropped. The alternative was to place him in a psychiatric hospital for $120,000 a year, where he would be far from home and where psychotropic drugs would be administered.

In this particular case, Tracey reports, the multi-faceted, community-based program worked. The young man is now much better, requires fewer services than he did at first, and attends a regular school.

Probation's Changing Role

Responsibility for young people who have shifted from Montrose and Hickey to community-based programs is shared between the NCIA staff workers and an "aftercare" probation officer. The relationship is not always easy. Probation officers regularly come to Tracey and say: "I told you so, the placement you found for this kid just caved in. Now what are you going to do?"

While he is too much of a diplomat to deliver the message from an official position, Tracey spoke freely to an interviewer. Given the opportunity, he says he would like to say to a probation officer who raises such questions: "What have you been doing for the past twenty years except put these kids in institutions? That's nothing to boast about. It's better to take a risk and try out a few different programs until you find one that works."

Some probation officers are having difficulty adjusting to their new role. Maryland's efforts to lower the population of its last remaining training school leaves probation officers with fewer institutional beds to incarcerate their charges in if the youths refuse to follow the rules of their probation.

"Probation officers are used to holding the 'big hammer' of Hickey over the head of kids and saying that if they get out of line they will send them back to the training school," Tracey explains. But now training school beds must be reserved for hard-core violent offenders, not for troublesome or obnoxious kids who won't listen to their probation officer.

Some street-smart kids have taken advantage of this change in policy. Realizing that they will not be reincarcerated unless they are rearrested, some now refuse to take drug tests or to abide by the curfew stipulated in the terms of their release. A few openly defy their probation officers, knowing that they will not be sent back to Hickey unless they are caught committing another crime.

It is difficult for probation officers who were accustomed to keeping a charge in line by threatening to send him back to the training school. "Now they have to be more inventive," says Tracey. Instead of threatening to return a youth to Hickey, the probation officer must develop a new kind of relationship with his charge and devise other incentives to get him to stick with his program.

"We burn a lot of energy keeping kids out of institutions," Tracey acknowledges. Finding people with the patience and commitment to work with kids who have a propensity for failure is difficult. But for those who come to know the inside of a training school like Montrose—where investigators encountered, for example, the case of an 11-year-old boy committed for stealing a bike who was raped by older boys—the advantages of small, community-based programs are obvious.

TAKING STOCK: ACCOMPLISHMENTS AND UNFINISHED AGENDAS

"Can adjudicated delinquents be safely moved out of the training schools?" Tracey asks rhetorically. "Yes. Unequivocally. I think we have proved that here in Maryland."

As evidence of Maryland's success in closing down one training school and reducing the population at another without jeopardizing public safety, Tracey points to recidivism data collected by NCIA over the course of their contract. Of the 117 Montrose residents who were returned home with services or placed in community-based programs over a period of 18 months, 30 percent were re-arrested, and of these youth, 22 percent were recommitted to juvenile institutions or waived to the adult correctional system.

"I think those figures will compare favorably with any other program in the country," Tracey observes. Certainly it is better than the previous Montrose recidivism rates, where 85 percent of committed youth were either referred back to DJS or were readjudicated within two years of their release from 1983 to 1985.

Similarly, the outcomes of transfers out of Hickey are also favorable when compared with the training school recidivism rates, Tracey continues. Of the 75 Hickey residents that NCIA returned home with services or placed in community-based programs, 14 (19 percent) have been recommitted to institutions or waived to adult court over an 18-month follow-up period.

Thus, most youths transferred out of the training schools stay out of the criminal justice system. That does not mean, however, that success comes easily or in every case when a youth is assigned to a community-based program. Tracey points out that at any given time some 20 percent of the deinstitutionalized young people have either run from their program or are having significant difficulties. It is part of NCIA's task to find new placements or to make program adjustments for those youths who experience difficulty in their community placement.

That a good number of young people continue to make trouble once they return to the community should come as no surprise, Tracey argues, nor should it be cause to reinstitutionalize them because they are found guilty of committing another crime. "The kids come to us with 14 years or more of personal history. Those years of chaotic family life do not just go away. You don't turn that around in one year. We may be able to change some self-perceptions and some attitudes. We may even inhibit some impulsive behavior. But we cannot erase the early abuses and victimization they have experienced during their lifetime. The disturbing news to some is that we can't 'fix them'. The problem will not go away," he continues.

"Even the best programs may fail with some of these kids. But the only hope for working with them effectively is what we call 'unconditional care.' That means we reject their delinquent behavior but we don't reject the person. We try to go beyond the traditional destructive response which says that because you have been bad we are going to treat you badly. . . . Tragically, our correctional history and current practices dictate that the only way to punish someone is to put him in a cage," he adds.

Criticized from Both Sides

In any public debate over how adjudicated delinquents should be treated by the state, opinions are bound to differ and emotions run high. As chief administrator of the state's juvenile justice system, Linda D'Amario Rossi is at the center of this storm in Maryland.

Not surprisingly, she is now being criticized from two sides of the deinstitutionalization debate. One set of critics faults her for not locking up enough kids in secure facilities; another group questions her plans to increase the number of secure commitment slots. These proponents of community-based facilities are asking why she has stopped short of closing Hickey and are disturbed by her ten-year plan that calls for retaining up to 216 beds in a combination of existing, rebuilt, and newly constructed cottages on the training school grounds.[6]

Why Not Close Hickey?

Why can't Rossi close Hickey and create small, secure commitment facilities around the state, following the lead of Massachusetts and Utah? Some argue that she is missing a historic opportunity to rid Maryland of its last remaining training school.

Controversy continues to swirl over the state's ten-year plan for juvenile facilities, which calls for retaining 72 beds in existing cottages at Hickey, building a 48-bed cottage immediately, at a cost of approximately $3.2 million, and investing another $6 million in 96 beds to be built in the future, at a total cost of some $9.2 million. Clearly, the proposed investment in rebuilding Hickey is substantial and arguably could be better spent on smaller, secure commitment facilities.

The argument can further be made that investing money to rebuild Hickey is not sound because the scale of the facility is too large and does not lend itself to the creation of an environment that promotes rehabilitation. Furthermore, operating costs at Hickey will remain high compared with the smaller secure commitment facilities slated for construction. When all 216 beds are on line in the rebuilt Hickey campus, operating costs are projected to total $11.9 million a year or some $55,000 per resident a year (compared with the current $60,000 per resident). In contrast, operating costs at the smaller facilities are projected at $39,000 a year per resident.

Tracey believes that continuing to operate Hickey is a waste of taxes. For the $60,000 spent every year per resident, he points out, taxpayers receive little more than the assurance that the youth is not on the street: the youth is kept under limited discipline and control, has a roof over his head, is fed, and receives some minimal educational services. "But very little therapeutic is going on at Hickey. It is exclusively control-focused," Tracey contends.

Of equal concern is that there is no differentiation in treatment at Hickey. A youth who needs $5,000 worth of services and a youth who needs $85,000 worth of services are both treated the same way. In contrast, Tracey suggests, the state receives a better return on its investment when it sends adjudicated delinquents to community-based programs where the level of care can be matched with the level of need.

"We showed when we closed Montrose that we could take the money and dispense it out to vendors who provide alternative programs for the kids," he explains. Officials in some other states remain skeptical about whether good private providers can be found to work with delinquents in the community setting. But the experience in Massachusetts, Pennsylvania, Utah, and Maryland demonstrates that if an invitation is issued to providers to create programs, and if money is available, plenty of competent providers will emerge, Tracey observes.[7]

So why is Rossi investing a significant portion of her construction and operating budgets in Hickey? The primary obstacle to doing away with the institution, she explains, is that it would entail a long, drawn-out fight to obtain permits to site replacement facilities in other parts of the state. If she became bogged down in a "not-in-my-back-yard" fight over locating facilities, it would delay the construction of well-designed secure commitment facilities. That in turn would impede her ability to convince judges to send to DJS a portion of the juvenile population that is currently being waived to adult court, she explains.

Rossi claims that if she had her choice, she would build smaller secure facilities to replace those at Hickey. "Do I want a 200-bed facility [like Hickey]? No. Do I understand that compromise is necessary without compromising our major mission? Yes. Hickey is one of those compromises.

"I get frustrated by these critics who say we haven't gone far enough," Rossi observes. The Hickey population has been reduced and the ten-year plan calls for removing the current "detention population" out of Hickey, and retaining only 216 "commitment population" beds.

"Right now Hickey has the potential to house 620 residents. I think our building plan will eliminate that possibility. At the end of the plan there will be only 216 beds. We will tear down the rest," Rossi promises. Each new cottage built at Hickey will hold no more than 48 young people in four modules of 12. Furthermore, for every new cottage that is built an old cottage will be destroyed, she explains.

Rossi argues that her compromise of keeping 216 youth at Hickey is, in effect, preventing worse proposals — including one for housing 300 residents there, and another for transforming it into a 500-bed facility operated by a private contractor. Rossi has opposed these proposals, arguing that there is no need for a facility of this size, and that establishment of the 500-bed facility would inevitably drain money away from the budget for smaller, community-based programs.

Ten-Year Plan

The debate over whether to close Hickey is not the only issue that concerns proponents of community-based systems. They also object to DJS plans to increase secure commitment capacity to 350 beds by 1995 and to 540 beds by the year 2000 — more secure commitment capacity than the state really needs, some argue. Were these plans to be carried out, DJS would need to build six smaller facilities around the state, in addition to the beds at Hickey.

Rossi disagrees. She does not believe that the plan would create an excess build-up of secure beds. She cites the following factors driving the need for more secure commitment beds:

• *According to DJS projections, the number of young people at risk of being committed to DJS will increase by 20 percent in Maryland over the next ten years.*

• *An estimated 300 to 600 youth are waived from the juvenile to the adult court every year. DJS administrators hope that their plans to build more high-security programs over the next ten years will tempt more judges to keep serious offenders in the juvenile justice system rather than transfer them to the adult system as is the current practice.[8]*

• *DJS plans to gradually increase the average length of stay of youths in secure commitment facilities from the current average of 4.5 months to 10.5 months over the next ten years, increasing significantly the need for secure commitment beds. The current length of stay does not permit time for a program of rehabilitation to work, Rossi argues. Critics, however, suggest that increasing the length of stay in a training school such as Hickey will not promote rehabilitation.*

To those who suggest that Rossi's plans to expand secure care represents a return to the "lock 'em up" system of the past, she replies: "I think it is unfair to say that we are going backwards. We are never going back to the policies of locking kids up in secure care in the kind of institutions we had in the state in 1987. We will not do that. Our plan does not allow us to do that."

Are the Streets Safer?

Have the extensive changes in Maryland's juvenile justice system paid off in terms of recidivism rates? Rossi explains that to date there is no good recidivism study of the Maryland system. To remedy this she has raised foundation money to do a comparison of recidivism rates before and after Maryland's deinstitutionalization drive. She expects the study to be completed by 1991.

Despite the lack of hard data, Rossi remains convinced that the new system she has ushered in is superior to the training school model. "Are the streets of Maryland safer? My gut feeling is that they are, because there is more dignity in the system and there is a better sense of values about how kids should be treated."

This survey of the impetus for change and the implementation of change makes it clear that the transformation of Maryland's juvenile justice system is still in progress. The debate will continue over whether Hickey should be closed and over the question of whether Maryland needs all the secure commitment beds it projects for the year 2000.

What can be said, however, is that Maryland has made significant progress in reducing the number of youth in training schools and broadening its spectrum of community-based programs. For this the Department of Juvenile Services deserves considerable credit.

[1] Maryland's Department of Juvenile Services was formerly the Juvenile Services Agency.

[2] The best description of how Montrose came to be closed is contained in a paper entitled "Youth Corrections in Maryland: The Dawning of a New Era," by Jeffrey A. Butts, in *Youth Correction Reform: The Maryland and Florida Experience*, Center for the Study of Youth Policy, School of Social Work, University of Michigan, September, 1988.

[3] The source for the following statistics is Virginia Miller, Director of Planning, Research, and Information Services at DJS.

[4] David Tracey now works at Family Advocacy Services in Baltimore. NCIA was founded and is directed by Jerome Miller, who closed Massachusetts' training schools during his tenure as commissioner of the juvenile justice agency in that state.

[5] These 117 residents were all that remained of a population of some 250 residents who were housed at the facility in recent years. The others had been moved out of Montrose prior to NCIA's involvement.

[6] Department of Juvenile Services, "Ten-Year Master Plan for Maryland's Troubled Youth: Executive Summary," January, 1990.

[7] Rossi notes that there were some problems convincing private providers to open programs for some delinquents. Some private providers believed that youthful offenders from training schools could not be properly handled in community-based facilities. In an effort to convince them that it was possible, Rossi sent some of them to visit programs that had been successful in Massachusetts. Despite these efforts, she had to bring in some out-of-state program operators to run programs for some of Maryland's delinquents.

[8] While judges who waive juveniles to the adult system may expect them to serve time in prison, in fact, some 225 of these waiver cases ended up being placed in an adult probation program. By applying Hickey intake criteria to this population, DJS administrators project that their increased secure-commitment capacity will permit them to house the majority of these young people. The ten-year plan calls for DJS to house 35 of this waived population in its secure-commitment facilities by 1993, 75 by 1995, and 150 by 2000. Source: Virginia Miller, Director of Planning, Research, and Information Services for DJS.

Utah Builds a Community-Based System

Fifteen years after a lawsuit drew attention to abuses in Utah's juvenile institutions, the state has transformed its juvenile justice system into a national model on the leading edge of reform.

In 1975, the St. Louis-based National Juvenile Law Center and the Utah office of the ACLU brought a lawsuit charging the state with widespread abuse of young people incarcerated at the 450-bed Youth Development Center (YDC), a reformatory that had been in operation under a number of different names for 80 years.

The year before the suit was filed, Jim Marchel, a researcher for Utah's juvenile court, began collecting complaints about YDC from the parents of juveniles held at the training school. "Some of the complaints were horrendous," Marchel recalls. "There was one allegation that a girl had been kept naked in an isolation cell for a month in a situation where male staff workers could look in at her."

Marchel also maintains that a "duker system" was in force at YDC under which some members of the staff enlisted the toughest inmates in the living unit to be their "enforcers." Handing over this kind of power to aggressive inmates resulted in weaker residents being subjected to extortion and beaten, he explains.[1]

"There was a lot of abuse of children going on in the system and people were worried about it," confirms Sue Marquardt, program coordinator at Utah's Division of Youth Corrections (DYC). "The system was locking up nine-year-old runaways. There were cases in which young Indian girls were locked up for promiscuity," she recalls. The court later appointed Marchel as "master" of the reformatory, to see that abuses such as this were eliminated.

The lawsuit against YDC was critical in pushing state officials to consider humane alternatives to the large warehouses they had been using, observes Youth Law Center director Mark Soler. A second lawsuit, concerning the misuse of detention in Salt Lake City, revealed that only five percent of the young people locked in detention were incarcerated for serious or violent crimes. The settlement in this case, *D.J.R. v. Christean*, set strict guidelines concerning the detention of juveniles in Salt Lake City. "As a result of the settlement, local officials had to develop a much broader array of community-based programs than was previously available," Soler continues.

"These Facilities Don't Work"

"YDC was charged with housing too many kids, improper use of isolation cells, and allowing members of the staff to read the kids' mail," recalls C. Ronald Stromberg, former director of the Division of Youth Corrections, who has recently been appointed director of the Office of Social Services that oversees DYC. Prior to his term as director of DYC he served as superintendent of Youth Development Center several years after the lawsuit was filed.[2]

"There was nothing malicious going on at YDC when I came there in 1978," Stromberg insists, "but we weren't doing a lot for the kids either. No one was concentrating on making the kids a whole lot better. The people who worked there just wanted their shift to go smoothly and then go home." In a sense, the staff had become as institutionalized as their wards, he adds.

"Those of us in leadership positions were saying that these [large training school] facilities didn't work and that we couldn't manage large numbers of kids in dormitories because all we ended up doing was concentrating on control," Stromberg continues.

Control became the paramount issue — to the exclusion of treatment — for obvious reasons, he explains. "The kids who were sent to YDC had initially been arrested because they couldn't get along with people on the outside. So naturally if you put 20 or 30 of them together in an open dorm they are going to fight with each other. The large training school was a ridiculous model for handling these kids. All you could do was try to control them and hope that no one got hurt."

Looking for a New Model

Advocates of reform in Utah's juvenile justice system found the class action lawsuit against YDC a blessing in disguise. "The lawsuit helped because we could go to legislators and tell them that they had a choice: either they could be clobbered in court or make a change in the system," Stromberg contends.

The support of Governor Scott Matheson for closing the training school and creating a community-based system was also a critical factor in making the transformation possible. An important motive for the governor's decision to make the transformation of the juvenile justice system a high priority was that he did not want the federal court to dictate how Utah ran its juvenile justice system. Instead, he insisted that Utah clean up its own act.

To avoid a court-controlled system, Governor Matheson appointed a blue-ribbon task force to examine Utah's juvenile justice system and look for ways to improve it. During this process a political consensus developed that change was both necessary and possible.

The direction of that change was established when Jerome Miller was called in to talk about his experience closing the training schools in Massachusetts and implementing a community-based system. Miller contended that the same model that worked in Massachusetts would work in Utah. Other juvenile justice experts who were brought in for consultation agreed.

Principles Guiding Reform

The emergence of two important themes helped create a consensus for reform: that a community-based system would cost the state less money; and that young people who have broken the law should be treated differently from adults who have done so.

Thus the decision to move to a community-based system was not entirely altruistic in its motivation. "Our decision was based in part on the very practical perception that building more training schools would be fantastically expensive. At a certain point you have to ask whether building more of the same is the smartest use of the money," Stromberg observes. He points out that a community-based system costs less per youth than the institutional approach. "Our budget stayed pretty flat during the transition to the new system. Now we spend the same number of dollars as before, but we serve more kids and serve them better than when we had them in institutions," he says.

In addition, Stromberg notes, the state came to realize that youths who go to training schools exhibit a high rate of recidivism, creating the necessity to build more facilities. "The legislators see that there is a vicious cycle: kids who go to training schools keep coming back, requiring the building of more facilities."

A consensus to adopt a progressive model for juvenile justice in Utah was forced only because the strong argument was made that young people who have broken the law should be treated differently from adults. "We argued that rehabilitative programs could have a positive impact on kids and the legislature agreed," Stromberg recounts.

However, Utah's change in policy on the treatment of juvenile offenders has not spilled over into the way the state's correctional system handles older adolescents or adults. For example, the legislature refused to allow the same community-based sanctions approved for juveniles to be applied to "youthful offenders" aged 18 to 22. These young men and women, once convicted of a crime, are treated as adults and are sent to jail or prison. Utah continues to hold a "lock 'em up" attitude about adults, and its high-security adult prison system continues to expand, Stromberg adds.

Building a New System

The steps Utah officials took to transform a training school-based system to a community-based system are best described by Van Vleet, Rutherford, and Schwartz in a paper entitled "Reinvesting Youth Corrections Resources in Utah."[3]

As these authors report, two separate blue-ribbon task forces recommended state policy changes that would lead to the most rational and humane system of juvenile justice. These recommendations, which were subsequently implemented by the state, included the following:

• *A Division of Youth Corrections should be established.*

• *Whenever possible, the agency should place youthful offenders in the "least restrictive setting" appropriate for their treatment.*

• *Status offenders—such as runaways and truants—who had previously been locked up with more serious offenders, should no longer be under the jurisdiction of the juvenile court.*

• *The department should establish strict criteria for the use of secure care. The number of secure-care beds should be limited to three 30-bed facilities built using funds generated from the sale of the YDC facilities.*

• *Youth requiring a lower level of security would be held in a decentralized system of community-based programs run by the private sector.*

• *Regional, non-secure observation and assessment programs should be established to replace the assessment program operating at YDC.*

• *Commitment and release guidelines should be developed to ensure that youth are sent to the appropriate program and released in a timely fashion.*

Even with these sound principles agreed upon, Utah confronted the problem of how to close the training school while at the same time opening new community-based programs to accommodate those leaving YDC.

The strategy employed was to close the facility incrementally by breaking down the training school population into small units. Each youth was interviewed to determine whether he or she should be required to remain in a high-security facility. Youth for whom a lower security classification had been approved were transferred into a unit at YDC before being moved as a group into the growing network of community-based, alternative group homes. The depopulated unit was then closed down. Funds previously used to support YDC residents followed them to the new community-based programs. In this fashion YDC was closed unit by unit, until the last inmates were transferred out in December, 1983.

The Courts Cooperate

The transition from the training school system to the community-based model required a good deal of cooperation between the new Division of Youth Corrections and the juvenile court. The juvenile court continued to have the power to decide whether a youth should be placed in a community program, an observation and assessment unit, or in one of the new 30-bed, high-security facilities. Had the court continued to make the majority of placements in high-security facilities as opposed to the staff-secure community-based programs, the system would have broken down. Preventing this were the strict criteria that had been agreed upon defining the criminal history of young people who should be sent to high-security facilities.

As the system evolved, a joint juvenile court and DYC screening committee evaluated adjudicated delinquents and made recommendations to the judge as to their disposition. "The screening committee would meet and say to the judge that Johnny should be placed with Youth Corrections for community alternative placement because he has certain treatment needs and certain supervision needs," Stromberg explains. With these recommendations in mind the judge would then make his or her decision. "Usually they agreed with the screening committee," Stromberg notes.

From the judges' point of view, the evolving system of juvenile corrections in Utah was an improvement over the training school model because it gave them more options in terms of where they could place a youth.

Unlike the old system, where status offenders and property offenders were mixed with youth convicted of serious, violent offenses, the new system involved more differentiation and allowed the majority of youth to be served in non-secure, community-based programs.

UTAH'S PLACEMENT OPTIONS

*S*tromberg is convinced that the only real hope for rehabilitating young people is to cycle them through a community-based system. "If you are really going to change a kid's life, you have to do it in the community with a lot of structure and supervision. I think you can hold kids more accountable in the community than you can in a high-security institution. For kids in large, high-security facilities, the institution lives their life for them. The staff wakes them up, they are told when to eat, when to go to school, and when to go home. Under these circumstances, the kid isn't learning any responsibility or accountability. If you want to make them responsible and accountable you have to get them out in the community. I'm not saying that every kid should be in a community program. There are some who are too dangerous for that and they have to be locked up. But something like one percent of the referrals to juvenile court end up in a secure facility."

A key feature in making the system work is the screening session that precedes a decision about the disposition of each youth.

Screening Sessions

One of the most impressive aspects of the Utah system is the way state officials manage to keep many troubled youth out of the criminal justice system. In many states, young people are committed to correctional facilities and programs for reasonably minor offenses that should be regarded more as due to deficiencies in their home environments and upbringing than as deliberately criminal acts. Once enmeshed in the criminal justice system, labeled as a delinquent and incarcerated with more serious offenders, these young people often embark upon a lengthy criminal career. Utah seems to avoid this pattern wherever possible.

At the Salt Lake City Juvenile Court a group of professionals — among them probation officers, members of the court's intake staff, a representative of the Division of Youth Corrections, and a representative of the Division of Family Services — screen cases that have come before a juvenile court judge prior to disposition. The object of the screening is to help the judge decide whether a young person convicted of breaking the law should be (1) placed on probation, (2) committed to the custody of the Division of Youth Corrections, (3) committed to the custody of the Division of Family Services (DFS), or (4) certified as an adult and sent to adult court. The idea is that these professionals are most familiar with the spectrum of resources available, that they have had time to review a young person's record in some detail, and that they can help the judge direct the juvenile offender to the program or facility most appropriate to their needs.

Specifically, the options from which the professionals and the judge can select for each youth range from secure care for youths who require confinement to various types of small, community-based residential programs, to non-residential services.

Secure Care

For young people who must be locked up, Utah has built three secure facilities with a total capacity of 70 beds, one in each of the state's three regions: the Millcreek Youth Center (30 beds), Decker Lake

Youth Center (30 beds), and the Southwest Utah Youth Center in Cedar City (10 beds).

Limiting the number of secure beds was intentional. In Utah these small secure facilities are prescribed only for the most violent and chronic offenders. In FY 1989, a total of 91 youth were committed to these secure facilities. Each of them had previously been convicted of an average of 33.4 offenses. Forty percent of them had one or more life-endangering felony convictions.[4]

A great deal of thought went into designing Utah's secure care facilities. Having found that in large facilities residents were taught to be good inmates, not good citizens, Stromberg became convinced that secure facilities that would have a chance of teaching chronic offenders to be good citizens should house no more than 30 to 40 residents.[5]

In addition to being small, secure facilities in Utah are designed to be hard on the outside (i.e., secure), but soft on the inside. Carpets on the floor are used to keep noise levels down, individual rooms are provided for privacy, and residents cook their meals and eat together in the facility. Even the furniture is chosen to give the facility a home-like look.

By creating as normal or home-like an environment as possible and staffing the facility with workers trained in crisis intervention, it was hoped that disciplinary problems could be minimized. The effort has proven largely successful, Stromberg reports. Instead of using isolation cells for behavior control, the staff do one-on-one counseling with residents who are being disruptive or send them to their rooms to "cool off." Only in very rare instances — two or three times in the past five years — have isolation rooms been used.[6]

A deliberate attempt is also made to use every opportunity within the facility to teach residents skills they will require once they leave. For example, residents must apply for a job within the facility and go for a "job interview." Similarly, if they want to purchase something at the in-house canteen, they have to use a "checkbook" and balance their account.

Decker Lake

One of these new facilities, the Decker Lake Youth Center, a one-story, tile-roofed, no-nonsense structure located outside of Salt Lake City, was opened in 1983. The emphasis here is in working with very disturbed young people in the smallest groups possible. With a capacity of 30 youth, the Decker Lake facility is broken down into three living units or "pods" of ten beds each.

Residents stay at Decker an average of eight months. The day is divided into seven periods, with academic work scheduled in the morning. Youths who come to Decker are an average of four grades behind where they should be chronologically at school. At Decker they receive highly individualized attention to help them catch up. In addition, each youth carries with him during the day a report card with comments written in by his teachers and counselors about how he behaved and performed during each period. "We cut through a lot of denial that way," one counselor observes.

Delinquents confined at Decker are frequently confronted by members of the staff, not only for anti-social behavior, but also for "criminal patterns of thinking." During the day group meetings are held, focusing on drug and alcohol treatment and social skills development.

One of the more refreshing aspects of Decker is the lack of an institutionalized split in the staff between teachers and living unit counselors. At many facilities, the teachers, social workers, and psychologists are seen as the professional staff, while the youth counselors who work on the living units are looked down upon as little more than correctional guards. At Decker, however, a serious effort has been made to encourage teachers to follow their pupils back into the living unit after classes and participate in group counseling sessions. It is also a matter of policy that teachers and administrators are just as responsible for confronting negative behavior and maintaining security as the youth counselors are. This makes the "team approach" more than simply a laudable, theoretical concept.

The prognosis for chronic offenders such as those housed at Decker Lake is not promising; most are convicted of offenses after their release. Two studies by DYC in 1986 tracked for one year youths who had been paroled from secure facilities the year before. Only 25 percent remained crime-free. Some 17 percent were convicted of misdemeanors and 58 percent were convicted of felonies. The only good news was that although half of these youths had previously been convicted of life-threatening felonies, during the follow-up period none were. While these recidivism rates may appear discouraging, it is important to realize that Decker serves a "residue population" of offenders whom most people in the system have given up on. Stromberg says that the judges who sentenced these young people to secure care have expressed surprise that so many of these youths remain crime-free for a year after their release from the secure care program.[7]

Observation and Assessment

Rather than sending some of the most serious offenders to high-security facilities, every year the department sends some 165 of the most disturbed young people committed to DYC to one of the department's three "observation and assessment" units.

Observation and assessment (O/A) programs are located in each of the three state regions. Delinquents with serious or chronic offenses are placed in O/A facilities for a 90-day assessment, during which treatment plans are devised. During the assessment period, each youth in the O/A center undergoes a psychological, educational, and vocational evaluation as well as a family history and a description of the youth's adjustment to institutional life.

About 20 percent of those who enter O/A go on to serve time in one of the state's three secure facilities. The others are dispersed to less secure community-based programs.

At the O/A program in Salt Lake City, youth are housed two or three to a room and are subjected to intensive counseling and monitoring. They are taught "anger management" techniques, given classes about victim awareness, and exposed to information from Planned Parenthood. Occasionally, if they have been well behaved, they are taken on brief trips outside the facility. Once they have finished their two- to three-month stint at O/A they are returned to the court for reassignment.

"This program is so highly structured that it is very uncomfortable for these young people," observes Bob Hefferman, director of O/A in Salt Lake City. "It causes them to stop and examine themselves." Young people who act out while in the program have the door to their room taken off its hinges and are assigned staff workers to "shadow" them until they calm down.

Group Homes

Most youth who are committed to DYC never go to a secure program or to Observation and Assessment. Instead they are routed to a group home or are sent home on parole with in-home services. The Larus group home, for example, admits clients 11 to 16 years old for an average stay of four months.

Jim Marchel, director of Larus, says that his program accepts youths who have committed a violent offense, first-time sex offenders, and arsonists, but will not admit young people who suffer from psychosis.

At Larus two counselors are always on duty. There are lots of outside activities for clients, including weekend skiing trips, which Marchel claims help instill middle-class values. Three times a year, longer trips are scheduled to Yellowstone Park or to Disneyland.

"There are always a few hard-core, sociopathic kids you get who will end up failing and are sent to an institution. But most of them eventually go home and live marginal lives. They do not become model citizens after they leave this system. We don't cure many of them. But we do show them how to move through society legally. We take them to plays and on other excursions that teach them how to have a good time without being arrested."

Odyssey House

Another group residence, Odyssey House, is located in a large, whitewashed residence in Salt Lake City with four pillars out front. Well-respected for its work with 13- to 18-year-olds who have been committed to DYC for crimes stemming from substance abuse, Odyssey House works primarily with youths who have been arrested for possession of drugs or burglary.

The program is not set up to deal with hard-core, violent kids, explains director John Eden, so an effort is made to screen out young people who exhibit psychotic behavior or are guilty of arson or sexual abuse. If a youth becomes violent he is forced to leave. "We call the police," he explains.

But Odyssey House has demonstrated that it does work for a number of young people with substance abuse problems. The program requires that residents must submit to a urinalysis test at least three times a week to see if they have taken drugs. Some of the counselors are ex-drug addicts who can relate to the problems of this particular group of young people. Residents stay an average of nine months, but some stay up to two years.

The program is highly structured and packed with individual, group, and family counseling sessions. Youths go through an initial orientation during which their family history, needs, and goals are assessed. During the "treatment phase," residents pass through freshman, sophomore, junior, and senior phases in which positive peer pressure is used as a motivational tool. Residents then move on to a "reentry" phase where they are prepared for their transition back into non-institutional life. Odyssey residents also attend their own alternative school in a building located two blocks away.

A central issue in many group homes is that young people who join the program frequently walk out the door when the program begins to make demands on them that they find offensive. At Odyssey House, one-third of the residents run away during their first three months in the program. "Usually kids run a few times before they settle down," Eden observes, but most get caught or come back on their own.

Proctor and Tracking Services

Group homes are not appropriate for all youth, Stromberg cautions. "There are some kids for whom positive peer pressure in a group home works well. But there are others who get in trouble in groups," he explains. Many of the youths for whom the group homes do not work are older adolescents who have already served time in more secure facilities.

For these young people a "proctor program" has been devised so they can live a semi-independent life in an apartment setting with a person, sometimes a college student, who acts as a combination roommate and role model.

The proctor's job is to provide a stable home for the youth, to give him good advice, and to see that he abides by the rules of the house—no drinking or drugs. But the proctor is not expected to follow his charge around town and make sure that he attends classes or goes to work.

That monitoring function is fulfilled by a "tracker," on call 24 hours a day, who makes sure the youth is either at school or at his job when he is supposed to be. In addition to their monitoring role, trackers also work as counselors, meeting with their clients a minimum of three times a week for a total of five to seven hours.

All of these services are overseen by a "case manager," who ensures that the youth is receiving the services that the state has paid the private contractor to provide. The case manager also keeps an eye out to ensure that the client is not being abused. Every three months, the case managers provide the court with a report about how a youth is doing in his or her current placement.

Case managers report two major sources of frustration. First, they find it difficult to locate residential slots for young people who do not abide by the rules. In Utah, a youth is locked up in detention only after he has run from his placement three times for 48 hours each time.

Debbie Rocha, a case worker for 2½ years, oversees a caseload of 17 youths. Of these, seven have run away and are listed as Away Without Leave (AWOL). "A lot of kids resent gradual release and feel that they have already served their time once they have been through Decker," she observes.

The unarticulated policy of DYC appears to be that while everything humanly possible should be done to reduce the number of youth who go AWOL from community programs, it is better to have them AWOL than locked up inappropriately for long periods of time in high-security facilities. Most youth who go AWOL are eventually picked up again and recycled through another program, the argument runs. Eventually they learn that they can run but they can't hide for long from the system. In the end, most of them realize that they are going to have to complete a community-based program before the system will leave them alone.

Transition Center

As Utah moved to a community-based system, the state found that some ideas that looked logical on paper have not worked out well in practice.

Chief among these was the notion that youthful offenders convicted of serious offenses should first be placed in the new 30-bed, high-security facilities, and then be integrated back into society after a stint in a group home and then a parole program. While this sounded like a sensible strategy for reentry — through a series of programs with successively lower levels of security and increasing levels of responsibility — it just did not work. Many youths who had served time in the secure facilities did not adapt well to group home living. The older adolescents objected to being grouped with much younger children and resented being required to abide by what they considered to be petty rules more appropriate to children. Many of them ran from these facilities or were soon rearrested on a new offense.

"In our first year out we had something like a 65 or 70 percent failure rate with kids who came out of our secure facilities," Stromberg notes. "We underestimated the problem of reintegrating them back into the community." Graduates from the high-security facilities did not do at all well in less secure group home settings.

Realizing that these young people required more specialized attention, DYC set up "transition centers" where they could receive intensive supervision and counseling during their first three months back in the community. Clients in the transition program receive a lot of attention from transition team workers who provide them with drug and alcohol counseling, help with schooling, finding jobs, community outreach and victim restitution.

But in addition to counseling and practical help in dealing with real-world problems, one of the most important functions of the transition program is to provide a temporary "crash pad" for youths in crisis who may be vulnerable to rearrest, and who need to get away from their home or neighborhood for a while.

Vendor System

With 446 youth served in community residential programs in 1988, and some 200 youth receiving non-residential services, the private sector role in accomplishing DYC's mission is now well established.

In the past, DYC contracts to the private sector were determined by competitive bid. A fixed-dollar contract was signed with each provider to keep open a specified number of beds in their facility or slots in their program. Inevitably this meant that the state paid for some beds that remained vacant. Faced with diminishing financial resources, DYC implemented a "vendor system" in 1986 whereby the agency now pays providers only for services actually used. This vendor system has its advantages and disadvantages.

"I don't think we could have started with a vendor system in the beginning," Stromberg notes. "A certain period of subsidy was necessary to get programs up and running." But now that DYC's relationship with private providers is well established, a more competitive system is warranted, he maintains.

Because it is impossible to predict the exact needs of the young people committed to DYC, Stromberg explains, the agency required the flexibility to identify the program that will provide the best supervision and treatment for each client. Under the new vendor system, he suggests, the best programs will receive support and expand—because DYC will send more clients to them—and the worst will have to fold because they do not receive enough placements to pay the bills.

While this sounds like the "American Way" of tough, capitalist competition in the marketplace, some providers see it as inherently destabilizing. They suggest that some good programs that fail to receive enough placements may be forced to let experienced workers go or to close down group homes. Then, they point out, if the client population expands the next year, the programs will no longer exist, the building will have been sold, and the experienced workers will have taken other jobs. "It might be better if they gave us some kind of subsidy during lean times so that we will be around when they need us," says Larus director Jim Marchel, whose program is just barely making ends meet.

THE UTAH EXPERIENCE

*U*tah has taken major strides by removing juvenile offenders from inhumane institutions and creating a multi-faceted series of community-based facilities and programs for them.

The positive effects of Utah's reforms emerge when the system is examined from at least three different perspectives: the number of youths deinstitutionalized and placed in community-based settings, the state's success in limiting the number of youths assigned to high-security facilities, and recidivism data.

On the question of movement out of institutions and into community-based settings, the data tell the tale:

• *The number of youths in high-security facilities dropped from 350 in 1976, to 200 in 1980, to 144 in 1988.*

• *The number of youths in community programs rose from approximately 20 in 1976, to 100 in 1980, to 250 in 1989;*

• *By 1989 there were 51 community-based programs on the state's list of approved contractors;*

• *In 1989, residential community-based programs served 485 youth; on a typical day 163 young people received services;*

• *More than 200 youths—an average of 65 per day—received non-residential services in 1989.*

Keeping the Numbers Down

Because delinquent youth are by definition "behavior problems" and potentially dangerous, there is a natural tendency to place them in the most secure setting available. One of the perennial problems in youth corrections is preventing the assignment of too many youths to high-security facilities.

Utah addressed this issue of controlling the proliferation of secure facilities by creating both "front end" and "back end" mechanisms to ensure that only youths who must be locked up are placed in these facilities, and that they are released from them as soon as possible.

At the front end, the DYC and court screening committee recommends to the judges which young people they think are appropriate for this highest and most expensive ($114 a day) level of care. Other clients may go through a 90-day observation and assessment unit before a decision is made to place them in secure care.

At the back end, a five-member citizen parole board, appointed by the Board of Youth Corrections, determines when a youth will be released from secure care into a monitored parole program. Other states, such as California, have had problems with parole boards that keep young people in high-security facilities longer than is appropriate, thus exacerbating the crowding of these facilities.

In Utah, however, the problem appears to have been solved. First, the parole board is given "guidelines" as to the appropriate period of time youths should serve in secure care for a variety of offenses. About 95 percent of the time the parole board goes along with these guidelines, Stromberg observes. If a bottleneck develops and the parole board refuses to release enough young people to prevent overcrowding in the facilities, there are two measures that can be taken. First, the director of the DYC has the authority to discharge any youth under an early release mechanism. In practice, however, he has never had to exercise this ultimate authority. Instead, when facilities are approaching overcrowding, he can send the parole board a list of the youths in secure care, ranked by the seriousness of their offense and their length of stay, indicating those he thinks are the least risky ones to release. The parole board then can pick from the list who they think should be released first. The director has some influence over the parole board's composition, because he screens applicants for the board prior to the final selection by the Board of Youth Corrections.

Recidivism

Perhaps the most important indicators of progress are the recidivism data, which suggest that Utah's new system is a significant improvement over the old one.

107

"The kids are doing better under the community-based system than they were at YDC. They feel better about themselves. But that doesn't mean they are pure, clean kids now. I don't think we have found any cure for delinquency. But I do think the new system is an improvement and that everyone is better off now — the kids, the staff, and the community," Stromberg notes. But even if there had been no improvement in recidivism and the statistics had stayed the same, the new system would still be an improvement because it is more humane, he adds.

Making this argument is unnecessary, however, because the recidivism data — both from the DYC itself and from an outside organization — look good. "Before they come to DYC our kids have committed an average of 13.8 misdemeanors and 4 felonies. In the year after they leave us they commit an average of 3 misdemeanors and 1 felony. Furthermore, 95 percent of DYC graduates with a previous history of violent offenses are violence-free during the year after leaving the agency. But a lot of them are caught for minor offenses such as trespassing and shoplifting," Stromberg continues.

A 1988 DYC study revealed that:

• *43 percent of youth terminated from custody in FY 1987 remained free of criminal conviction during their DYC custody;*
• *Of these, over 75 percent were conviction-free for a year following their release;*
• *When DYC youth did reoffend, there was a significant reduction in the overall volume and seriousnesss of their criminal activity.*"[8]

In addition, a study by the National Council on Crime and Delinquency (NCCD) found that while large numbers of DYC offenders continue to be arrested for crimes (53 to 81 percent), there are large declines in the rate of offending in the year following release from DYC programs. "The 247 Youth Corrections offenders in the NCCD study accounted for 1,765 arrests in the 12 months previous to their commitment to the Division. Once released into the community, these same youth accounted for 593 new arrests — a drop of nearly 66 percent compared to the pre-Youth Corrections period."[9]

The report also concludes that the data strongly indicate that "the imposition of appropriate community-based controls on highly active serious and chronic offenders did not compromise public protection." Furthermore, "youth with lengthy arrest records can be safely returned to the community after relatively short periods of confinement under a well-funded community corrections program," the study concludes.

Better than Most

It is not difficult to find fault with correctional systems, and Utah's is no exception. Recidivism data, while encouraging, still indicate that large numbers of youth are rearrested following their release from the system, albeit at a slower rate and for less serious crimes than under the old system. The number of youth who run away from community-based programs also remains a matter of concern.

Nevertheless, compared with juvenile justice systems in many other states, what is happening in Utah is incredibly civilized. In a span of ten years, the state has managed to develop a spectrum of humane and safe programs and facilities for juvenile offenders. This is no small feat. Adopting a few basic principles and sticking with them has brought about a radical improvement in the way juvenile offenders are treated.

Chief among these principles are the following:

• Large training schools don't work.
• A decentralized spectrum of facilities is needed to fit the needs of a diverse population.
• The least restrictive environment possible consistent with a reasonable definition of meeting public safety goals is the best policy.
• Private sector involvement in the creation of programs for youthful offenders can be successful.

Nationally, the political climate has made it difficult to convince legislators to vote for alternatives to incarceration for juveniles. Nevertheless, Utah's Stromberg predicts that the community-based model will eventually prevail. "Research will prove that the community-based system is superior to the training school model," he forecasts.

One compelling reason to adopt the community-based model, Stromberg continues, is that decentralizing DYC services allows committed youth to remain closer to their families. By distributing DYC programs around the state, Utah has made it possible for the families of committed youth to be more involved in their rehabilitation. Working with young people in their community of origin also facilitates a more gradual transition back to the community once they are released. "Since we are keeping youth closer to their own homes, we can involve everyone in the treatment process," Stromberg adds. As a result, sometimes it is possible to improve the environment that a youth returns to upon release. To those who say that the Utah system can only work in a small state with a manageable number of juvenile offenders, DYC director Stromberg suggests a decentralized approach. California, for example, has a bigger juvenile offender problem than does Utah by several orders of magnitude. However, if the administration of juvenile justice in California were divided into subdivisions, he suggests, the same approach could work. "There is no reason that a city like Fresno could not do much the same thing that we have done here in Salt Lake City," he concludes.

[1] In his excellent monograph entitled Out of Harm's Way (Edna McConnell Clark Foundation, 1988), Richard Margolis further details abuses that were commonplace at YDC prior to the lawsuit.

[2] Tim Holm has replaced C. Ronald Stromberg as director of DYC.

[3] For a more complete history of juvenile justice reform in Utah see "Reinvesting Youth Corrections Resources in Utah," by Russ Van Vleet, Andrew Rutherford and Ira M. Schwartz, in *Reinvesting Youth Corrections Resources: A Tale of Three States,* Center for Study of Youth Policy, School of Social Work, University of Michigan.

[4] Utah Department of Social Services, Division of Youth Corrections, Annual Report, 1989, p. 21.

[5] Stromberg, Ronald C., "Accountability and Treatment of the Serious and Chronic Juvenile Offender," in *Programs for Serious and Violent Juvenile Offenders,* Center for Youth Policy, School of Social Work, University of Michigan, Nov., 1989, p.17.

[6] ibid.

[7] ibid.

[8] Division of Youth Corrections, Annual Report, 1989, p. 26.

[9] National Council on Crime and Delinquency, "The Impact of Juvenile Court Sanctions: A Court That Works," January, 1988.

Florida Reduces its Training School Population and Supports Some Innovative Community-Based Programs

The problems Florida confronted in its juvenile correctional system by now will sound familiar. In 1983 the state faced a class action lawsuit *(Bobby M. v. Martinez)* charging that crowded and unwholesome conditions prevailed in Florida's four major training schools, which held 847 delinquents. Subsequently, two training schools were closed, but the other two remained open.

By 1987 a decision was made to resolve the suit through a negotiated settlement. In the consent decree that followed, Florida officials agreed to substantial reform of the system, including drastically reducing the number of young people in the two remaining training schools.

Today, the combined number of youth in Florida's two remaining training schools — the Arthur G. Dozier School for Boys and the Eckerd Youth Development Center— has been cut to 266, and further reductions are scheduled.

Despite this impressive reduction in the institutionalized population, a number of juvenile justice experts involved in moving Florida towards a community-based system suggest that the state still has a long way to go. Both the Youth Law Center and the ACLU National Prisons Project have threatened the state with contempt proceedings in order to push development of community-based programs, notes Mark Soler, executive director of the Youth Law Center.

While the Bobby M. consent decree effectively slashed the number of youth in training schools, the political climate in Florida has caused large numbers of youths to be tried in the adult courts and incarcerated in adult prisons. Furthermore, adequate funds have not been invested in a full spectrum of community-based programs.

111

Reform Movement Stumbles

The move toward a community-based system began during the 1988 legislative session, when over $5 million of new money was appropriated to build up community-based programs that were to form the core alternative to the training schools, recalls Samuel M. Streit, the former Director of Children, Youth and Family Services, Department of Health and Rehabilitative Services. This boded well for a real change in the system. "We had ambitious plans for reforming the system; we had a grand vision," Streit remembers.

But the bottom dropped out of these plans for reform the following year when it became apparent that there was no political consensus to do away with the remaining training schools and move to a community-based system. Streit and others lobbied hard to close the Dozier training school and use the funds saved through its elimination to beef up the community-based programs.

But the opponents to closing the training school, particularly the legislators from the district in which Dozier was located, put together a winning coalition. They argued that the state was plagued with "thousands of brutal and vicious juveniles and that closing training schools did not make sense," Steit recalls.

Unable to close Dozier and move the money into the community-based system, state juvenile justice administrators found themselves between a rock and a hard place. On the one hand, they could not increase the number of delinquents sent to training schools because of the Bobby M. consent decree; on the other hand the legislature was unwilling to appropriate more funds to expand community-based programs.

The state addressed this double bind by trying to make adjustments with existing resources. The first change, according to Streit, was to shorten the average length of stay for youths in community-based programs. For example, delinquents were sent to halfway houses for three months instead of six. This allowed more delinquents to be cycled through the system, but inevitably the rehabilitative efficacy of the programs suffered.

Another "adjustment," made by judges and prosecutors, was to increase the number of delinquents transferred to the adult court from some 3,700 in 1987 to more than 5,000 in 1989. Ironically, observes Streit, many of these youths sent to adult court do not end up serving time in an adult prison. Many beat the charges against them because they are better represented as adults than they would have been as juveniles. Others are released on probation after serving time in jail waiting for their court appearance.

Nevertheless, 929 juveniles were sent to adult correctional facilities in 1988, notes Paul DeMuro, a court-appointed monitor of the Bobby

M. case consent decree. In contrast, Massachusetts, with approximately half the population of Florida, sent only 16 juveniles to adult corrections.

The transfer of large numbers of juvenile offenders to adult courts and correctional facilities is troubling to many observers in the state, who are well aware of the potential for juveniles to be abused by older, tougher inmates in adult facilities. Until this practice can be significantly modified, Florida will be a long distance from providing adequate programs and facilities for its juvenile offenders.

Despite these less than progressive aspects of Florida's juvenile justice system, Streit argues that there are many positive characteristics of the system that should not be ignored. For example, large numbers of young people are diverted from the juvenile justice system at the district level into Juvenile Alternative Services Programs (JASP), "one of the best such programs in the country," Streit maintains. Similarly, Florida's school-based delinquency prevention programs are among the best in the nation, he continues.

Finally, while the state has yet to close its last training schools and commit adequate funds to the development of alternative options, some of the most innovative community-based programs in the country have come out of Florida. Two of these, operated by the Associated Marine Institutes, are described below.

Associated Marine Institutes

At first blush the idea sounds far-fetched — one might almost say reckless. Imagine, if you can, taking a group of inner-city delinquent kids and teaching them scuba diving, sailing, navigation, fishing, powerboat handling, and boat repair.

The possibilities for calamity are without number. Skeptics would argue that working around boats in drydock or on the ocean is no game for kids — particularly impulsive, irresponsible, undisciplined, assaultive, and certifiably criminal young people. Nightmare scenarios are easy to imagine: kids might drown (and one has), boats might be stolen or hotrodded around the harbor, expensive fishing gear and diving equipment might disappear.

But in another sense the ocean/delinquent match-up seems curiously congruent. Adolescents with strong tidal rushes of hormone-induced emotions surging through their systems may find a certain relief in wrestling with something larger than themselves — the power of the sea. Coming to terms with the immensity and power of the ocean may help put personal problems in perspective. The notion of "going off to sea," even if only experienced in a very peripheral sense, can capture the adolescent imagination.

113

Working around boats also has the collateral advantage of generating an enormous number of roles. One can work one's way up from swabbing the deck to captain. One client can drive the boat, another can take care of the engine, a third can handle navigation, a fourth can be in charge of fishing and diving equipment, and a fifth can be cook. Assigning roles to troubled youth, in a warm and caring environment that includes some real-world challenges, can foster a sense of positive identity that has been lacking in their lives.

Such are the theoretical underpinnings of Associated Marine Institutes (AMI), a nonprofit chain of 24 programs for adjudicated delinquents. First established in Florida, AMI has spread to Texas, Louisiana, South Carolina, Delaware, Massachusetts, Virginia, and Maryland.

AMI is one of the best-known and respected networks of community-based, non-institutional programs for delinquents in the country. Operating since 1969, AMI has developed its own ocean-based techniques for working effectively with young people. These include enriched water-related recreational activities for young people, used as a reward for sustained academic work and good behavior; a vocational program that is attractive to many young people; a level system and token economy; and a priority on finding school and job placements for its clients after they finish the program.

AMI strives as assiduously to motivate its staff as it does to motivate its students, even pioneering by establishing a profit motive for improving the quality and "productivity" of its programs. Staff workers who help a certain number of their students pass through the program with positive results are rewarded with dollar bonuses that can increase their salary by 10 to 15 percent. Not surprisingly, these financial incentives make the staff persevering and results-oriented in their work with these young people.

"We run our business like a business," explains Bob Weaver, executive vice president of AMI. "If a program runs better than an 80 percent success rate with its students, it will show up in the staff wallet in cash money. And if they don't, it won't."

Tampa Marine Institute

A visit to Tampa Marine Institute (TMI), located in an industrial sector of Tampa near the docks, gives a sense of why AMI works so well.

Parked on the lawn outside the facility is an old tugboat, signaling the nautical focus of the project. Inside, a harpoon mounted on the wall of the muster-room further expresses the seagoing theme.

At 9:30 a.m. the backless wooden benches in the main meeting room are crowded with an assortment of young people, long of hair and generally of a mien that signifies their reluctance to be present at this

114

required morning assembly. Counselors stand at the front of the room near a flag and lead the students in the Pledge of Allegiance and a prayer.

What follows resembles a cross between a revival meeting and a football rally. Counselor Ray Jackson, himself once a delinquent youth, leads the students in energetic clapping and foot stamping that makes the room resonate like a drum. At Jackson's instigation, the group claps and stamps to welcome a new client to the program, then to welcome back to the fold a client who has skipped out of the program for the last week. They also clap and stamp to hear about a range of recreational activities, including a deep-sea fishing trip they can purchase a berth on, with points earned through attendance at the program, completion of academic assignments, and cooperative behavior while at the program.

While the clapping and stamping appears falsely enthusiastic to an outsider, it does have the effect of riveting everyone's attention and making them march in the same direction. To generate this kind of activity, the staff must be energetic, and TMI staff workers are. They appear to be motivated to see clients in their charge perform well.

Academic improvement among students is a high priority at AMI. In various AMI programs, clients move up one to four grade levels in the six months they spend in the program. In addition, approximately half of the students eligible earn high school equivalency diplomas while at AMI.

One reason for the success of the academic program is a staff ratio of one instructor to seven students. But equally important is the way the program makes academic skills relevant. Half of the student's time is spent in the field receiving "hands-on" instruction. This breaks up the classroom monotony and clarifies the real-world application of various lessons. For example, if a student wants to learn how to repair a power-boat engine, then he must be able to read the manual. If he wants to be able to navigate the boat, he must learn basic mathematical computations. And if he wants to go snorkeling or scuba fishing, he must learn how to identify fish.

Macho Vocational Role Models

The "marine" aspect of the program is really the bait to hook the interest of the client. Since most AMI programs are unlocked day programs, they must use a clever combination of carrot and stick motivators to entice young people to participate. Without locks on the doors, students who don't like the program can simply walk away and tell their probation officer to find them another program.

"If a kid comes to the program for two weeks we can usually hook him on it," observes Michael Atkins, program administrator at TMI.

"We welcome the kid with open arms and try to give him a relaxed feeling about being here. We try to make kids want to be here by rewarding those who complete academic work with attractive vocational and recreational activities," he continues.

Nautical instructors appeal to the kids as being sufficiently macho role models. Most adolescents find it easy to develop a relationship with the seamanship instructor, who teaches powerboat handling, sailing, and fishing. Motivating a kid to learn to drive a motorboat is about as difficult as convincing him to test-drive a motorcycle. By the time newcomers to the program see TMI's sailboat and two powerboats (one 21-foot and the other 25-foot), most are intrigued enough to give the program a try.

The aquatics instructor, who teaches swimming and life saving, and the diving instructor, with his tanks, wetsuits, flippers and goggles, are also appealing figures. Teaching inner-city adolescents how to swim and scuba dive challenges them to do something they have never done before and makes them learn a skill that gives them confidence that can spill over into other areas of their lives. Even the vocational instructor, who teaches outboard engine mechanics and boat repair, has a certain appeal for a number of these young people. (AMI solicits donations of boats, which the students then repair for use in their program or for resale.)

Each client who enters the program is also assigned an advisor, who will stick with him through good times and bad. The advisor is charged with getting to know the student and his family better than anyone else on the staff, as well as helping to set goals that the student must accomplish before graduating. He is responsible for ensuring that everything possible is done so that the client benefits from the program. One responsibility of the advisor is to call and check on clients who do not show up in the morning. If the call doesn't produce an adequate answer, the adviser will visit the student's home to learn why he failed to attend.

"We have to learn to distinguish between what is just normal adolescent behavior and signs of real trouble. When a kid is really acting out, we try to look for the underlying cause. Some of these kids live in incredibly difficult circumstances. We try to come to an understanding with the kid and his family about what his real situation is like and then work from there," Atkins observes.

An example of this is the story of a TMI graduate who landed a job and was then arrested for breaking into the store where he worked. An investigation of the break-in revealed that the young man was sleeping in the store at night because his home life was so chaotic that he was afraid to stay at home.

"These kids require a lot of individual attention. You also have to be fair and consistent with them and show them that you love them," Atkins adds.

Incentives

AMI uses a token economy and a level system as behavior modification mechanisms. Students earn points through their record of attendance, attitude, behavior, and achievement. These points can then be spent to "buy" a variety of excursions, for example, a berth on a four-day fishing trip to Panama Key. Or they can be used to purchase a sweatshirt or other treats. The point system also doubles as an efficient way to teach clients how to manage a budget.

As students earn points, they also rise through the nautical ranks from deckhand, to bosun, to ensign, to helmsman. Each promotion comes with a new hat, which the student can wear to flaunt his rising status. Privileges and responsibilities also come with promotion. The longer a student has been in the program, the more is demanded of him in terms of controlling his own behavior and setting a good example for the other students. He must also meet a number of short- and long-term goals for self-improvement.

With these new responsibilities come corresponding benefits. For example, when the deckhand becomes a bosun, he becomes eligible to drive his own car to school or to accompany the staff on trips to a convenience store. Promotion to ensign qualifies the student to spend only a half day at the program on Friday and another half day of on-the-job training. The helmsman is eligible for full-time, on-the-job training and is allowed to go on any and all trips.

Population Characteristics

This system of behavior controls and motivators has been designed to work with very troubled male and female adolescents. More than 90 percent of the young people who enroll in TMI are felons. Typically, they are property offenders with related drug and alcohol abuse problems. TMI accommodates up to 50 adjudicated young people, ages 15 to 17, over a minimum period of six months. TMI does accept some violent offenders, and serves some youth returning from training schools, but will not accept arsonists or murderers.

About five to ten students out of a class of 40 do not make it through the program, explains one TMI counselor. Others require more than six months to complete the program. "Some are here up to eight months. We stick with some of the kids who are the most troubled. We go all out for them. We come to work every day believing we can succeed with them. You can't just be a baby-sitter here. We want to put out a good product," says the counselor.

When a student leaves the program, an advisor helps him find a job or return to school. For six months following his release from an AMI program, a community coordinator helps the youth work out problems with his parents, boss, or teachers. The progress of the youth is then tracked over a three-year period.

Recidivism Rates

AMI has proven remarkably successful in rehabilitating youths who go through its institutes. Between 1969 and 1987, some 12,500 young people completed AMI programs. Of these, 80 percent have had no negative contact with law enforcement since they left the programs.[1]

"Our success rate in these programs has been good. Four out of five of our kids are not adjudicated again. And these are kids who previously were burglarizing houses and knocking people over the head. Now they don't. I call that success," Atkins declares.

AMI is not shy about celebrating its successes. Graduation ceremonies, complete with caps and gowns, are held every month, and are frequently attended by a youth's parents, judge, and probation officer. The graduate gives a speech, receives a diploma, and has his graduation ceremony videotaped.

Bob Weaver, executive vice-president at AMI, argues that one of the advantages of AMI non-residential programs is that they teach young people how to live outside the institutional environment.

"In the typical training school, a kid gets up when someone tells him to, he eats when someone tells him to, he goes to the bathroom when someone tells him to. Then when he is released from the institution and he doesn't know how to catch a bus, all the experts can't understand why. Obviously the kid didn't learn life skills while he was in the institution," he observes. In small, community-based programs there is a better chance of equipping young people who have committed crimes with the skills they need to survive without breaking the law, he concludes.

FLORIDA ENVIRONMENTAL INSTITUTE

Fish Eating Creek seems a curious location for a work camp for youthful offenders convicted of serious crimes. The 40-acre site is set deep in a Florida swamp, 40 miles northwest of Lake Okeechobee, and 25 miles from the nearest signs of civilization. In addition to being remote, the area is hot, humid, and infested with alligators, snakes, and man-eating mosquitoes.

Yet in some respects, the harsh conditions and remote location of the Florida Environmental Institute (FEI), operated by the Associated Marine Institutes (AMI), are advantageous to the program's mission.

The remote location and alligator-inhabited swamp make escape from the facility difficult and hazardous enough so that no security fence or locked doors are necessary. The harsh conditions and demanding regime of hard physical labor also provide FEI's 22 residents with an incentive to perform well in the program, so they can graduate to more comfortable circumstances.

Since it opened in 1982, FEI has been used by the state as a "last chance" for young men convicted of serious crimes who might have been sent to adult prison had this alternative not existed. "We ask the judges not to send us a kid unless all the other possible alternatives have been tried," explains Bob Weaver, executive vice-president of AMI.

As a result FEI receives young people that other programs would just as soon avoid. "These are hard-core, long-term, violent kids," Weaver continues. Seventy-five to 80 percent of the residents at FEI have been convicted of a violent crime ranging from attempted murder or rape to assault. The program does not accept adolescents who are drug-addicted, mentally retarded or sex offenders. On average, residents spend approximately a year at the work camp. "This program is not for everybody," Weaver observes. "We don't take aggressive homosexuals, for example."

The experience of being "sent up the river" to what the residents call "the Last Chance Ranch" is intentionally used as a way of impressing on those committed to FEI the seriousness of their crimes. Sending them into the swamp is a surefire way to get their attention. For inner-city kids, the experience can be more than a little scary. Many young men who are tough on the street and bullies on their own block are terrified of the wilderness, wild animals, and an unfamiliar environment.

The arrival of a new resident in camp is carefully choreographed, notes FEI executive director Michael Dulin. The resident's initiation begins with a hike from the highway through the outback to a primitive camp. The newcomer is accompanied on this trek by a counselor who will be his advisor. The new resident spends his first three to five days in "orientation camp" ten miles from the main facility, where he is schooled in the rules of FEI by key members of the staff and senior residents. The rationale behind orientation camp is that it helps the new resident bond with key members of the staff. The hope is that if a strong relationship is established from the outset between advisors and the resident it may prove easier to direct the youth's rehabilitation.

When the new arrival is brought into camp, he is paired up with a resident who is nearing graduation. The veteran resident is assigned the task of introducing the new young man to the program and providing a positive role model. The incentive to the veteran resident to do a good job is that it will count toward his release.

Life at FEI is far from the typical custodial experience. Students are expected to clear the swamp, build the facility, attend academic classes, and work on their own rehabilitation.

When students arrive at camp they are placed on "Level One," and live in a primitive, barracks-like wooden building constructed by previous residents. The floor is poured concrete and the decor is cinderblock and painted or unpainted plywood. Each resident sleeps in a double-decker bunk bed and stores his few possessions in a plywood footlocker secured with a combination lock. Large screened windows, without glass, are equipped with wooden covers used when a storm comes in. There are several ceiling fans.

The hardest work is clearing land for beef cattle, a task made grueling by the combination of heat, humidity, and mosquitoes. Residents also learn to do the carpentry, plumbing, and electrical work required to complete the as-yet-unfinished facility. A point and level system is used to monitor a student's progress and to provide incentives for good behavior and hard work. The fact that there is no relief from the heat and humidity makes this behavior modification system work better than most.

An important incentive for performing well at the work camp is to move out of this sweatbox into an air-conditioned trailer which is reserved for those who reach "Level Two." Students must amass a large number of points before graduating to AC comfort, by working hard at all assigned tasks, being polite and well behaved, and attending classes. Students on Level Two are also permitted to watch television, make more telephone calls home, have opportunities to earn money off-site, and receive parental visits. Other rewards include taking a student off-site to the nearest town for a restaurant meal.

"The better a kid behaves, the more time counselors spend with him," notes Michael Dulin, FEI's executive director. Those who misbehave may be assigned to a work detail digging stumps out of the ground from 8 a.m. to 5 p.m. Those who are found guilty of serious misbehavior (fighting) are sent to "disciplinary camp"—a tent set out in the wilderness. There they must do hard physical labor all day, under the supervision of a counselor, and then sleep in the tent at night.

Sending kids who act out to disciplinary camp turns out to be the least restrictive way of dealing with the problem. "We have no lock-up room at FEI and we don't teach our staff to 'take kids down' by wrestling them to the ground and pinning them. We are convinced that the more unusual you treat a kid, the more unusual he will act. We don't treat these kids any different than we would treat our own children," Weaver observes.

Finding staff who can keep young people with an assaultive history under control without resorting to physical confrontation is not always easy, Weaver notes, particularly in a rural area in Florida where corporal punishment is a widely used child-raising technique. "In Florida there were 140,000 kids paddled last year in the school system. Here corporal punishment is the norm, and I'm in the business of looking for people who don't want to whip their kids," he says.

That does not mean that punishment is not used in AMI programs. "We believe in punishment," Weaver continues. "But for the punishment to work the staff member has to have the kid's best interest at heart, have the punishment fit the crime, and the punishment must be in a time frame the kid can understand."

The Cook Gets a Vote

One of the more effective aspects of the system is that the entire staff votes on whether or not a student deserves to move up to the next level, and any one staff member can block the promotion. The fact that the cook has a vote, as well as the counselors, administrators, and teachers, makes the students treat everyone with respect.

Despite the hard work and primitive conditions at FEI, the overall atmosphere is not punitive. Many of the residents express a sense of accomplishment at having met the challenge of surviving under these conditions. They are proud of the ground they have cleared, of the buildings they have built, and of their academic achievements. A spirited student-staff volleyball game, for example, has significance beyond recreation; the students had dug the pit, filled it with sand, and erected the net. The fact that the students have a sense of "ownership" about the program makes it particularly effective.

Aftercare

Thirty days prior to graduation, a student is awarded a gold cap symbolic of his elevated status in the program. During that month, the student is encouraged to make more decisions for himself and to demonstrate that he can handle the responsibility. Once the student graduates to "Level Three," he returns home but continues to be seen two to three times a week by one of FEI's four community coordinators. On "Level Four," the community counselor makes one visit a week.

"At FEI the kids get intensive aftercare attention, not just some help. We continue to assist them for up to six months. Our community coordinators have a caseload of eight and see these kids face to face a couple of times a week. They help them with their family, help them get food stamps if they need them, intervene for them with their boss if they are having trouble on the job. And they do counseling with the kid on nights and weekends," Weaver explains.

Overall, AMI manages to place 88 percent of those who finish their program either in school or in a job. But the problem is not just finding a job, Weaver observes — it is helping the adolescent keep the job. "Our kids don't get fired for job-skills reasons. They get fired because they don't come to work or because they have a lousy attitude. As a result, each aftercare worker has to help each kid in a different way. One kid may need help buying work clothes or hard-toed boots. Another may need to be taken to a doctor to get a physical or helped to get a driver's license."

Recidivism

Not surprisingly, recidivism rates for those who go through the FEI program are not as impressive as the 80 percent success rate at AMI's non-residential programs. Adolescents sent to FEI are among the most troubled youth in the Florida juvenile justice system, and success with this group must be measured on a different scale than success with the less serious offenders. FEI residents average 18.5 offenses and 11.5 felonies. Some 63 percent of FEI's referrals are for crimes against persons, while the remaining 37 percent are for property crimes.[2]

Forty-five percent of FEI graduates are recidivist, compared with a 60 percent recidivism rate at Florida training schools, Weaver observes.[3] Weaver defends FEI recidivism rates as acceptable, given the fact that most of these young people would have been sent to adult prison had it not been for FEI. "The kids who are sent to FEI are potential lifetime incarcerants, so if you are effective with one or two of these kids out of ten the long-term savings to the state are significant," he observes.

---

[1]It should be noted, however, that this sample is only of those clients who "successfully" complete AMI programs. It fails to take into account the 30 percent of those who initially enroll in AMI programs who are "negatively terminated." These include young people who repeatedly refuse to go along with the program and are expelled, those who are arrested for an unlawful act while participating in the program, and those who refuse to attend. If these clients are included, recidivism rates would be considerably higher.

AMI executive vice-president Bob Weaver notes that recently the state has been sending tougher kids with more prior adjudications to their non-residential programs. As a result, a number of AMI non-residential programs now have recidivism rates in the "high twenties and low thirties." Nevertheless, recidivism data from other sources suggests that AMI programs are remarkably effective. Statistics compiled by the State of Florida Department of Health and Rehabilitative Services, for example, shows that AMI programs in Florida are the most effective in the state at reducing recidivism. Recidivism occurs in some 33 percent of AMI students, compared to 60 percent of those in Florida training schools.

[2]Weaver, Robert S., "The Last Chance Ranch: The Florida Environmental Institute Program for Chronic and Violent Juvenile Offenders," in *Programs for Serious and Violent Juvenile Offenders.* Center for the Study of Youth Policy, School of Social Work, 1989, pp 36, 37.

[3]Here Weaver is referring to Florida Department of Health and Rehabilitative Services Outcome Evaluation Component statistics.

Conclusion

As we move into the 1990s, it is becoming increasingly apparent that, socially as well as financially, we can ill afford a correctional system that is inefficient, inhumane, and expensive. We must realize that young people who commit crimes are not "a breed apart"; they are our children, and we must work to help them now or pay the price in the future.

This monograph suggests that there are good programs within some state juvenile justice systems that are helping young people find a way to avoid institutionalization and teaching them how to live productive lives.

The upbeat tone of this report stands in stark contrast to much of the reporting about the condition of juvenile justice in this country. This accent on the positive was deliberate. If we do nothing but focus our attention on the problems in juvenile justice, we may overlook important programs that actually work. Learning to seek out, identify, and replicate model programs is a worthwhile exercise.

However, news of a growing network of good programs in states abandoning the training school model should be seen in context. Many states have yet to close their training schools, and some who work in the field of juvenile justice are impatient with the pace of reform.

In some circles, there is a sense that as a nation we are failing to take the necessary actions to keep our society from developing a permanent underclass that is kept under control by ever-rising rates of incarceration. There is concern that the underprivileged members of our youthful population will come to be seen by more fortunate Americans as a threat and not as a potential resource.

Some very savvy experts in the field of juvenile justice — while they admit that there are some good programs in a number of states — are depressed by the federal government's lack of leadership in helping the states move toward less incarcerative and more rehabilitative approaches to juvenile justice. They also see ominous signs in the proliferation of psychiatric in-patient units now being used as an adjunct to the juvenile justice system to confine young people who have a drug or alcohol problem, or who simply will not abide by their parents' wishes.[1]

The impatience of those who want reform to move faster is understandable. In a sense, training schools are like little factories that manufacture a bad product. Every year that they remain in operation, they put graduates out on the street who are both angry about the conditions under which they have been confined and who are ill-equipped to make a legal living or to interact with others in a civilized fashion.

Our training schools damage people who in turn pass their hurt on to others. Our penchant for incarcerating large numbers of young people transfers patterns of violence and other negative institutional values back into society when an overloaded, ineffectual system returns unrehabilitated delinquents to the street.

"Look at what is happening in Washington, D.C.," where the incarceration rate is now up to 1,700 per 100,000, urges Jerome Miller. When these delinquents emerge from D.C.'s training schools, he says, many carry with them institutional values they learned at Oak Hill: "The whole dealing, jiving, conniving way of institutional life is reproduced in the street." Having been "schooled-down" in the institutions, these graduates talk prison talk and walk the prison walk. In effect, they turn the streets of the city into one big prison yard.

There is hope, however, that we can break out of this cycle, which will only intensify if we continue to institutionalize youth unnecessarily. We have an opportunity to work at rehabilitating delinquents in small, community-based programs where there is a chance to teach them useful skills, and where outreach workers can secure jobs or appropriate schooling for them upon release.

Agenda for Reform

The preceding chapters suggest that juvenile justice systems can change, that training schools can safely be closed, and that the private sector, given adequate funding and oversight, can provide highly structured, community-based programs that create an environment much more conducive to rehabilitation than that which exists in training schools.

Changing the juvenile justice system in states that still depend on training schools as their main juvenile crime-control instrument will take perseverance. For this to happen, we must create a consensus that the system can be changed safely. Media coverage of the abuses that pervade many training schools can be useful in bringing about legislative reexamination of the juvenile justice strategy, or the filing of lawsuits.

But once the issue enters the political arena, it is important that key state policymakers, including legislators and the governor, be educated about the fact that viable alternatives to training schools exist. Sending a team of correctional officials to visit and observe the accomplishments in states such as Massachusetts and Utah can help convince key players that community-based systems are more than just a good idea — they actually work.

Beyond exposing legislators and correctional officials to model programs, it is important to assure the public that chronic and violent juvenile offenders will be appropriately confined in small, secure programs under the reformed system. Without this assurance that dangerous offenders are being confined, no community-based system can survive.

Furthermore, reformers must educate the public to the fact that community-based programs are not just "a slap on the wrist," or overly lenient. Good community-based programs are highly supervised, and every minute of a resident's time is organized and monitored. In the residential programs I visited, residents did not wander out of the building into the community without a counselor. In fact, in many of these programs, residents were not allowed to move from one room to another without permission. Thus, although there were no locks on the doors, the youths were, in effect, confined. And, as observed in several states, many community-based programs place more demands on residents than do training schools, where residents are confronted much less frequently about anti-social behavior.

The message that community-based programs are tough on delinquents, and constantly make demands on them to change their behavior, is a hard one to communicate to the public. It is only by extensive visits to both training schools and small community-based programs that the merits of abandoning the former and multiplying the latter become apparent.

By visiting training schools and talking with the residents, one finds that many delinquents who spend years in these facilities are learning the wrong lesson. Training school life teaches that the most aggressive and vicious residents hold the power in the crowded dormitories and dayrooms. This is not a lesson that translates well to the community after the resident is released.

In contrast, young people who spend time in small, highly-structured, community-based programs receive a lot of individual attention and counseling from members of the staff. They are constantly confronted about their behavior and motivated to change it. And they are introduced to new skills and experiences that will help them finish school, get a job, and get along with others once they are released.

The news that there are programs that work reasonably effectively with youthful offenders does not capture many headlines. Yet the problems of young people dealing or hooked on drugs or involved in acts of crime often does. The reason for this is that many people have a highly emotional reaction to juvenile crime, and it has been easy to manipulate this sentiment and to avoid serious discussion of what to do about delinquency.

"Delinquents have done something bad and should be sent far away to some place where they will be punished." This has long been our approach to juvenile crime. But it has not worked. Many delinquents emerge from training schools worse than when they entered.

Furthermore, by keeping delinquents out of sight, warehoused and iceboxed in distant, rural facilities, we avoid listening to what they have to teach us, notes Jerome Miller. Many youthful offenders have something important to tell us about ourselves and our society, he continues. If we have the strength and patience to deal with them in our communities, the story of their lives may give valuable hints about how to change the circumstances that breed criminal behavior.

After all, juvenile offenders are our children. They are not aliens landed from some distant planet. They are the product of our society. By our policies and practices we have helped shape them. This does not exempt them from responsibility for their criminal actions. But it does leave us with the responsibility to help rehabilitate them. This we must do, in our own self-interest as well as theirs.

Ultimately, the choice between the training school and the community-based model can be made by answering a simple but telling question: Where would you rather see your children serve their sentence were they convicted of a crime? After visiting both training schools and community-based programs, most people will have no hesitation in answering that the latter are far superior.

[1]See Ira Schwartz, *(In)justice for Juveniles: Rethinking the Best Interests of the Child*, Lexington Books, Lexington, Massachusetts, 1989, pp.131-147.